MAKING SENSE OF THE CHAOS

A Call to Action

Bobbie Stevens, PhD

BALBOA.
PRESS
A DIVISION OF HAY HOUSE

Balboa Press books may be ordered through booksellers or by contacting:

Balboa Press
A Division of Hay House
1663 Liberty Drive
Bloomington, IN 47403
www.balboapress.com
1 (877) 407-4847

Because of the dynamic nature of the Internet, any web addresses or links contained in this book may have changed since publication and may no longer be valid. The views expressed in this work are solely those of the author and do not necessarily reflect the views of the publisher, and the publisher hereby disclaims any responsibility for them.

The author of this book does not dispense medical advice or prescribe the use of any technique as a form of treatment for physical, emotional, or medical problems without the advice of a physician, either directly or indirectly. The intent of the author is only to offer information of a general nature to help you in your quest for emotional and spiritual well-being. In the event you use any of the information in this book for yourself, which is your constitutional right, the author and the publisher assume no responsibility for your actions.

Any people depicted in stock imagery provided by Thinkstock are models, and such images are being used for illustrative purposes only.
Certain stock imagery © Thinkstock.

Print information available on the last page.

ISBN: 978-1-5043-8220-5 (sc)
ISBN: 978-1-5043-8221-2 (hc)
ISBN: 978-1-5043-8232-8 (e)

Library of Congress Control Number: 2017909281

Balboa Press rev. date: 07/19/2017

CONTENTS

PART TWO—MOVING TO THE WORLD STAGE

PART THREE—WHERE WE ARE TODAY

DEDICATION

To my late husband Dr. Dean Portinga
and ALL Unlimited Futures Course Participants
and Supporters

ENDORSEMENTS

"Seldom do I find a book that rings so true for me. Bobbie Stevens' book, *MAKING SENSE OF THE CHAOS: A Call to Action,* should be required reading for everyone on our planet...Yes, it is that good!

> --**Ernie Carwile**, Author of *EVEN THE TREES WERE CRYING*
> www.ErnieCarwile.com.

"A timely and important book that synthesises and analyses the problems of today's world succinctly and clearly. Dr. Steven's book provides a welcome blueprint for a way forward recognising that a change in consciousness and a new approach is necessary if we are to successfully overcome the issues we are facing in a troubled world."

> --**Joe St Clair**, Managing Director
> 'The Laszlo Institute of New Paradigm Research'
> Global President of 'Eternea'
> Author and Speaker.

It's often true, action does speak louder than words. However Dr. Stevens' new book "Making

Sense of the Chaos" **screams bestseller** from beginning to end. This book provides the empirical formula to not only surviving in today's world, but succeeding. Dr. Stevens' book is an exceptional, motivational and enlightening book on change & inner spirit. Truly the best book I've read in a long time. Thank you Dr. Stevens.

--Dr. Eric Kaplan, 3 time #
1 Bestselling Author
"Lifestyle of Fit & Famous"
"The 5 Minute Motivator"
"Awaken The Wellness Within"
CEO at Concierge Coaches

"Making Sense of the Chaos is a powerful antidote to the chaos that we experience in our dynamic and chaotic world. Its principles outline a simple and clear path to a higher level of functioning that will change your life for the better.

--Jayme A. Check, CEO of
Quantum Global Partners,
Bestselling author of *The New Leader's 100-Day Action Plan*

Making Sense of the Chaos' vision, provides enlightening insights in understanding our own evolution, and attainable foresights toward how we can actively co-create a brighter future for us all.

--Rev Diane Scribner Clevenger,
Senior Minister, Unity of Naples

In Making Sense of the Chaos, Dr. Stevens explains what's happening in the world today, why it's happening and what we each can do to change it. This book offers a way to move into a more advanced level of consciousness and create a better world for all of us.

--**Marci Shimoff,** Professional Speaker
#1 *NY Times* Bestselling Author,
Happy for No Reason, Love For No Reason,
Chicken Soup for the Woman's Soul
www.MarciShimoff.com

"Since we are all connected, and what affects any us of affects all of us, we can create a world that works." That's the message of *Making Sense of the Chaos* and it is really great news for all of us concerned about the chaos in the world today.

--**Pete Bissonette,** President,
Learning Strategies

ACKNOWLEDGEMENTS

First I want to thank, my friend, Diane Fulbright, who has read and reread different parts of my manuscript and has given me invaluable suggestions. I also want to thank my friends, Rev. Diane Scribner Clevenger and Rev. Eileen Shaw who have also given me invaluable ideas and suggestions.

I want to acknowledge the great support I have received from my friend and business consultant/manager Patricia Maltz, who has helped me every step of the way in getting this book published and out to the public. My thanks also go to my business partner in Unlimited Futures, Michael Grubb, who has been supportive for many years.

My sincere appreciation to Bridget Egan and Juliana Nahas who are always there for me and support me in every way.

There is also a great group of people I would like to acknowledge who have all experienced our Unlimited Futures courses and are totally supportive in helping to get this book out and move this knowledge along to as many other people as possible. They are, Jayme Check, Amin Abdi, Anthony Ford, Alexis Spoiler Todd, Bridget Egan, Becky Amble, Alexander Larson, Carol

Murie, Jon Godfrey, Juliana Nahas, Kim & Tom Spudic, Vijay Venkatachalam and Michael Davis.

A special thanks also to my friend Ilke Marechal for her encouraging words and research.

I also want to thank Paul Sheele and Pete Bissonette for their continued support.

And I can't forget all the helpful people at Balboa – thank you.

And last, but not least all the people I have written about in this book who have provided so much valuable information for all of us.

INTRODUCTION

The ills from which we are suffering have had their seat in the very foundation of human thought. But today something is happening to the whole structure of human consciousness. A fresh kind of life is starting. There is for us in the future not only survival, but superlife.

-----Teilhard de Chardin,
The Phenomenon of Man

M AKING SENSE OF THE CHAOS is about something very special that underlies the total chaos we see going on in the world today. You can make a difference and the world needs your help.

Part I takes a quick look at where we find ourselves in the world today. We then start looking at what we can do about it. We look at why we find ourselves in this state of affairs. How it all came about and what we can do now. We discuss one huge misconception or incorrect belief that has laid the foundation for the myriad of problems that we are facing.

In Part One, we also take a look at what has been going on in the background that is leading us to a whole new understanding and experience.

Part Two is a look at what life could look like after the transformation takes place. I believe this transformation will be taking place in the world this twenty first century.

In Part Three, we look at how it all came about and options we all have for participating in creating a much better life for ourselves and a better world for all of us.

PART ONE

THE ONE INCORRECT BELIEF THAT UNDERLIES OUR MYRAID OF PROBLEMS

Chapter 1

WHAT'S HAPPENING?

If you do not change direction you may end up
where you are heading
Lao Tzu – 6th century B.C.E.

I THINK WE ALL KNOW that we do not want to end up where we seem to be heading.

The world needs your help!

What is happening to us – to our world?

- Almost every day in the news we learn of another mass killing that has happened in a school or a mall or office.
- We hear about people killing people on the highway due to road rage.
- Domestic violence is increasing.
- We are seeing a huge rise in addictions of all kinds.
- We are experiencing global warming - the glaciers are melting and the waters are rising.

- The weather has become erratic and large numbers of people are being killed by major storms, fires, flooding, etc.
- We see corruption in government, our legal systems, businesses etc.
- Terrorist are striking in different locations around the world on a regular basis.
- We see intolerance for people who are different from what is considered the norm.
- The language we hear in politics would have been unthinkable in the past. Politicians have always had differences of opinion but we could, at least, count on them to be civil in the past.
- It has now become acceptable to make up lies about someone and publish them in the media.
- Fake news is ramped – people believe these lies and act as though they were true.

How can we know what to believe?

What most of us would like to do is just ignore it all and go back to our lives as usual, but unfortunately life as usual doesn't exist anymore.

It would be comforting to think that one day things will go back to normal. Unfortunately what we have thought of as normal in the past is just that "past".

Let's look at what is happening. And most importantly what we can do about it.

I hear people all over saying, "I am just one person, "What can I do?"

There is much you can do. You matter – what you think matters.

Keep reading – I explain what's happening and how you can make a big difference in what you will be experiencing. And at the same time make a contribution to creating a better world for all of us.

FEAR AND STRESS

Fear creates stress and stress creates fear. It is a vicious cycle and it is going on in the lives of many people around the world. Actually stress is affecting all of us on a daily basis – just getting the news is stressful, but there is something we can do about it.

It is easy to understand how stress affects objects like wood or metal. We know that if we keep adding more pressure to a piece of wood or metal at some point it will break. This is also true of the human mind/body system, but somehow in our busy lives we have overlooked this fact.

When fear and stress become unbearable something has to give and numerous things can happen. It usually shows up first in mental and emotional malfunctioning. It certainly clouds ones perception. It can also show up as one's belief that someone else is responsible for their situation. One can become angry and want to punish whomever they believe is responsible. A person living in fear and sever stress is no longer able to see possibilities and can feel helpless and hopeless.

Fear, Stress and a totally incorrect belief are the underlying culprits in creating the world we see around us today. I won't go into details here about how stress affects us but I have written a book explaining it, entitled *Understanding Stress* and you can get a copy free on my web site at <u>www.unlimitedfutures.org</u>.

THE SOLUTION

We can see the problem and get some insight into the underlying cause, but what can we do about it? After all, individuals and small groups of people have used fear to control the masses since the beginning of recorded history. Fear is a very strong motivator.

I am going to show you how we can change that and make sure it never happens again.

Let's start by taking the advice of a very wise man named Albert Einstein. He gave us much good information while he was here and one of the things he said is that imagination is more important than knowledge. So, let's start by exercising our imagination.

Imagine that we are all in the spirit world where everything is so very beautiful and easy. We can just think of something and it automatically appears. We are having experiences and life here is good. We are just hanging out in bliss. Then there is an announcement asking if we would like to participate in a challenge. Wow, it has been a long time since we have had a challenge that sounds like fun, so we check it out.

We find out that there is a huge happening on earth and we have the opportunity to go there and be a part of it. We can decide who we want to be and what we want to do there. But, the challenge is, that when we get there, we will not be able to remember who we are or our previous life. Our challenge will be to discover who we are, why we came here, and what we are supposed to do here.

Life has been so good for so long, we are sure we can handle this and it will be fun. We are also told that if we do well in this challenge we will get a promotion when we get back home. We learn that if we do what we are supposed to do, we will be able to move into an expanded level of awareness.

So we sign up. We can see earth and the play going on but they can't see us. We look down and find a couple who will be willing to bring us into this world and take care of us. We pick a couple that seems ideal to provide us with the opportunity to play the part we have chosen, to learn the things we need to learn here. We know we need a body to get through this experience, so we create a body, a small one to facilitate our entry then we know we can grow it into the kind of body that will be perfect for our role. So off we go.

The first few years we are here we are just trying to get acclimated to this new environment. Our parents and the other people around us tell us how it works and what we should do. We spend the first few decades just taking in information and experimenting with how to fulfill our needs and desires. We, of course, are told how to do that by the people around us. So we believe what they tell us and move on. We go to school and get some more information about how it all works

Then at some point in time we take a look at our lives and start to think about it and if we have time to ponder it, we begin to have questions. These questions will come sooner or later but if we stay busy enough we can ignore them until something happens that finally gets our attention. That is what we are calling a "wake up call". We can all observe that we are getting a very loud wake up call right now.

I was at that point of questioning in my early thirties. I had done most of the things I had been told were the things to do to become happy and successful. I wasn't unhappy or unsuccessful, but there was something missing. I begin to look at my life and the people I knew, and thought, "There has to be more to life than this". "Could this possibly be all there is?"

Then more questions like, "Who am I?" "Why am I here" and "What am I supposed to be doing?" Have these questions come up for you yet?

If we pay attention when these questions arise and we begin to search for answers, we will find the answers. **After all this is our whole purpose for being here.**

If we just keep busy and ignore this feeling it will keep coming back in different ways until we do pay attention and begin our journey of discovering who we are and why we are here.

When I started looking at my life and asking these questions I had been questioning other people's beliefs for years, and found that most of the old paradigm, (world beliefs) simply did not make any sense to me. I knew there had to be more, there had to be a better way.

Most of the people I knew were running around like crazy, working day and night to make money. One day I saw a bumper sticker that said, "He who dies with the most toys wins". It got my attention and I had to ask "Why"? What's the money for? With enough money we can buy houses, cars, boats, airplanes,

anything we want, but what do we really want? At that mom
I knew there had to be a reason why we are all here, and I
didn't think it was just to make money and collect toys. Plus, I
already had all the material things I needed or wanted. I know
that if we don't have our basic needs met money is necessary
to meet them, but beyond that what good is money? It couldn't
buy peace, love or fulfillment and I realized that those were the
things that I wanted.

My burning question at the time was "What is life really all
about?" So, I became very quiet and said, "If there is a God,
then God knows I really want to understand how life works, what
it is really all about, why I am here, and what I should be doing"?

Shortly thereafter I found an article in a magazine about
some breathing exercises that were supposed to help one stop
smoking. I had started smoking when I became a flight attendant
or stewardess as we were called in those days. Smoking was
the "in" thing to do at the time. We even served cigarettes
with meals on flights. But I hated the fact that I was addicted
to cigarettes, and had tried to stop smoking many times. My
greatest accomplishment in that department was that I had quit
for two years, but a crisis came up and I was back smoking
again.

I located the author of this magazine article. She was a yoga
teacher. She taught me some breathing exercises, and also
some yoga stretching exercises. I wanted to exercise at home
between sessions and couldn't remember how, so I looked for
a book on the subject. At that time I also found a book on
meditation and focusing techniques. I put together a routine of
these things (stretching exercises, breathing exercises, meditation
and focusing techniques) that I started doing on a daily basis.

My whole life changed.

First, I quit smoking, and haven't had the slightest desire for a cigarette since, but that was just the beginning. My energy started increasing, and I began feeling younger and more confident. In time, somewhere between one and two years of starting my routine, I started noticing that I began to know things that I had no way of knowing. According to my nature, I started experimenting, and I found that I could get quiet, and ask a question and somehow I would get an answer to my question. I checked out my answers and they were right on, so I started asking bigger questions. I asked the questions that I had been pondering, "What is life really all about? How does life work, and what role do we each play in creating our own experiences?"

I had what psychologist, Abraham Maslow describes as a "peak experience". Maslow found in his studies that some people have what he called "peak experiences". He said a peak experience is when one can see the entire universe, understand its workings and knows his or her place in it.

I had such an experience. I saw the entire universe and understood how it works. I could see that the same structure is replicated throughout nature. However, I had no words, or any way to communicate what I knew. It was years before I could even speak about it at all. Now I understand what happened, and I will explain it later, but at the time I could only live from my new understanding, but couldn't put it into words.

When I asked, "Why am I here and what should I be doing with my life?" I clearly understood that each and every one of us has a purpose or reason for being here. I could see that each of us plays a role in the health of the universe. The answer that I received for myself, was that I was to share what had been revealed to me with others. I had no idea how to do that, but in time, it has unfolded for me.

Over time I did find words to help describe part of what I had experienced. It would take centuries to verbalize it all---- if that were even possible---- but the exciting thing for me is that over time I have watched science discover some of the same things that I could clearly see and understand years earlier.

I could clearly see that everything in the universe is connected. I could also see that there are laws of nature or principles of life that govern how it all works.

For some time now scientists have been exploring the mind and consciousness and have come to a whole new understanding of the workings of the universe. There is now undeniable evidence that the universe, including the world, doesn't work the way we have believed it did.

The major world belief is in separateness. Since we are individuals, in separate forms, it certainly seems that would be the case. But science has now clearly proven that the entire universe (everyone and everything in the universe) is connected. There is an energy that connects all of us and everything in the universe.

We could think of it as each of us being a part in a larger body. I could see that our physical bodies are a replica of the universal body.

As we know, all the cells in our bodies work together to support each other in creating a healthy functioning body. All the cells are individual cells but they know they are part of the body and they work in harmony with the other cells. They are intelligent and know their purpose in the larger body. When we know that we are all parts of a larger body then there is no longer an "Us and Them". We are all in this body together and we each have a function to perform for the good of the whole.

When we have an intention, say to take a walk. Many different parts of the body must perform (do their part) to carry out that intention. They all do so automatically working together to fulfill their purpose.

Because we have not understood that we are also part of a larger body we have believed what we were taught. We believed the science of our time which taught us that we were separate and on our own. We were taught that we must be better, smarter, stronger than others to make our way in the world. We have to be able to compete with others to prove ourselves. We must look out for ourselves even if it hurts others.

Science had it wrong and unfortunately we all believed what we were told and acted accordingly.

Just think how different the world would be today if each of us had known this one fact. Realizing this truth actually changes everything.

Take a minute to just think about it. Imagine how different our lives and experiences would be had we known that we are not separate entities, but understood that we are cells in the body of the universe.

Chapter 2

FUNCTIONING FROM A NEW UNDERSTANDING

Man's capacities have never been measured,
Nor are we to judge what he can do by any
precedents, so little has been tried.
> \- Henry David Thoreau

FORTUNATELY, SOMETHING VERY SPECIAL HAS been going on at the same time as the chaos has been created.

People around the world are having huge awakening and at this moment the universe is providing us with a giant leap in the evolution of human consciousness. Signs of this awakening have been appearing for decades now. And there is a reason why we are all here at this time in history. Together we will create a totally different world and you are an integral part of it.

Most of us are feeling overwhelmed with what's going on in the world today but, could it be that what seems to be happening **to** us is actually happening **fo**r us to help us discover the knowledge and power we have **within us**?

Has the world turned upside down to force us to take a look at ourselves and the beliefs we have entertained in the past? Is it time for us to start questioning the beliefs of the past and look for a deeper understanding of our lives and our world views?

As we know, we express our beliefs through our actions and our actions have consequences which are our experiences. As an example, I believe that I can jump off a bridge into the river and be just fine, so I act on that belief. My experience then will be determined by whether my belief was correct or false.

The same thing happens with our collective beliefs and actions. So what we see in the world around us today is the consequence of our collective beliefs and actions.

No matter how good intentioned the people who passed on their beliefs to us, it seems that they were simply wrong. They didn't know. They too were misguided. Science has just in the last few years discovered that our past world views were completely incorrect.

I believe that our new frontier is not outer space, but inner space. Is it time to start looking within ourselves, since we now know that we are a part of something so much bigger than anything we had even imagined before?

The exciting thing about this is that we can all be explorers. We don't have to wait for science to tell us about all the treasures we can find in our inner world. We all have complete access to this information simply by looking for answers to our questions within ourselves rather than seeking answers from an external source.

AWAKENINGS

Two major forces are influencing the world simultaneously, which we will look at in more detail later. There is a very powerful destructive force, destroying everything we have known in the past. And at the same time there is a very powerful progressive force that is moving us into expanded levels of awareness and knowledge.

Signs of awakening to the realization that things are not working the way we thought they did have been appearing for decades now.

Let's take a look at some of the things that have happened in the past to bring us to this level of awakening and where it could lead us.

During the 1950's, the noted psychologist Abraham Maslow gave us his famous hierarchy of growth. These are the states of consciousness that we all go through in our evolutionary growth process.

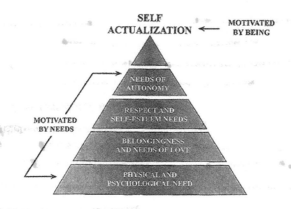

In his writings he explained that we all have needs and we must be able to fulfill our basic needs before our attention goes to higher levels of needs. Then as our awareness expands, we focus on a higher need.

Maslow says we are motivated by our needs. First we focus our attention on fulfilling our most basic physical needs like food, shelter, clothing, etc. When we are able to fulfill these needs our attention moves to our need to belong, to be accepted by others, to be a part of a group or community. Once we are secure in our ability to fulfill these needs, our attention moves to the need for respect and self-esteem. We need to know that we are competent and be recognized for our competency. When we feel secure in this area our attention moves to our next higher need which is autonomy. We want to be in charge of our own lives.

At this point we begin to realize that we are responsible for what we believe and start to question the programming we have received. We are no longer willing to simply do as we are told or follow the leader. We need to know that we can take charge of our own lives, and express our own talents and abilities.

Maslow also discovered that there were a few people in our society who had reached the top of the chart. They had been able to fulfill all of their needs and had become self-actualized. Maslow said these people were no longer motivated by needs. He did an in-depth study of these self-actualized people and found that they were the healthiest people in our society, they were also the happiest. They were highly creative, and highly intuitive. Most of them were also highly accomplished, and were involved in making a contribution to the world in their own way. Maslow said these people had discovered their ability to fulfill all of their needs right within themselves. He said these people were motivated by Being, which to me means that they had discovered the answers to their questions right within themselves. They had discovered their own inner self and the wisdom that we can all find there.

Maslow estimated that there were only a few people in the world functioning from this more advanced level of functioning at that time, but it was obviously a human potential and we were all moving in that direction.

In the 1960's, it became obvious that many people had evolved through the lower levels of Maslow's hierarchy. They had been able to fulfill their physical needs, their belongingness needs, their need for respect and self-esteem. They were clearly approaching their need for autonomy. Students in colleges across the country began to refuse to be controlled by fear. They were no longer willing to do as they were told regardless of reason. Students begin to stand up to authority, and, in essence, say "We are intelligent human beings, and we will make our own decisions. We no longer believe many of the things that we have been told and we will not continue to go along with many of these outdated beliefs."

The social activism of the late 60's and early 70's gave way to a different expression of change. People wanted to know themselves more. We saw many signs of this in business development courses, encounter groups, motivational speakers, consciousness-expanding weekends, inner child retreats, psychotherapy sessions, self-hypnosis techniques, getting in touch with emotion seminars, inter-personal relationship trainings, past life regressions, channeled entities, the re-emergence of religious worship and inspirational speakers.

There were thousands of workshops, books, retreats, lectures and seminars. Hundreds of thousands participated. And it didn't seem to make much difference whether these programs were permanently helpful or not. People flocked to these activities. The market of interested individuals was quite large and participation continued to build even though many of these programs didn't produce lasting results. The intense desire to just get in touch with a deeper part of ourselves was predominate in our minds.

This was a clear sign that many people in our society were feeling the need for autonomy, to be in charge of their own lives. Many were also asking deeper questions and realizing that there has to be more to life than what we have been experiencing, opening the door to self-actualization.

In 1980 Marilyn Ferguson wrote *The Aquarian Conspiracy*, a book that started a trend. Since then writers, social activist, psychologists and theologians have attempted to define and describe what this expansion of consciousness is all about.

Ferguson predicted the changes that are now happening. She had uncovered what she called an underground network of people who were working to create a different kind of society based on a vastly enlarged concept of human potential.

Ferguson writes, "There is incontrovertible evidence that we have entered upon the greatest period of change the world has ever known. We are the children of transition, not yet fully conscious of the new powers that have been unleashed."

She tells us that when a sufficient number of individuals have discovered and actualized this power within, a major paradigm shift will take place. The result of this more advanced level of functioning will begin to show up in all areas of our lives, and the world will be changed.

Today more and more people are becoming aware that we have all been hypnotized, by the beliefs of others. Our minds have been programmed, just like we program a computer, to believe what we have been told all of our lives. We are first exposed to our parent's beliefs, then our siblings, friends, teachers and most effectively now, the media.

Many people have a stake in what we think, what we believe and our behavior. We are becoming aware that if we simply accept what we are told without questioning it, we are simply perpetuating other people's beliefs, and aiding in the status quo. When we start taking charge and thinking for ourselves, discoveries are made and change takes place.

Governments, religions, businesses and others have controlled the masses through fear for centuries, and they have done a very good job. We have been programmed to believe that something terrible will happen to us if we even question the things that others have a vested interest in our believing.

Today millions of people around the world are waking up, moving beyond the fear and starting to ask questions about things that have never before been challenged.

Chapter 3

ARE YOU READY?

Each person is born with an infinite power, against
Which no earthly force is of the slightest significance:
Neville Goddard (1905-1972) philosopher

L ET'S TAKE A LOOK AT how it works and how we create our own experiences and contribute to the collective consciousness that creates the world we see around us.

We live in two different worlds. They are our inner world and our outer world. The outer world is where we do what we do and observe what others are doing. It is the material world where we observe all the things that are going on around us. And it is really easy to believe that it is all there is.

However, we also experience ourselves in our inner world. The inner world is where our innermost feelings and beliefs reside. It is also the source of our attention or focus. Here is where we decide what we want to do. Our mind and spirit resides here.

As our awareness expands we become aware that our inner world is causal and the outer world is the effect. The inner world creates the outer world that we experience individually and collectively. The inner world is where we find Nature and the laws of nature and principles of life that is expressed in the outer world. These laws and principles are absolute (non-changing). As we become aware of these laws and principles we understand how the outer world and our experiences are created.

All of the power lies in the inner world. When we know ourselves on this level we can create our outer world the way we want it to be. This is true due to our connection with the entire universe.

However, when we identify with the outer world we disconnect from the power that lies dormant within all of us in our inner world and we get blown about by life like a leaf and the wind.

As we become self-actualized we see the external world from a different perspective. We know how it came to be and we know that we can change our experiences. And together with others, as more and more of us become self-actualized, we will create a completely different world from what we see today.

Gradually we will see world beliefs and attitudes changing. The prevalent attitude of "What's in it for me?" will change to "How can I help?" Self-actualized people understand the law of giving and receiving. Giving and receiving are two sides of the same coin you simply can't have one without the other. The quote from the Bible that explains it, goes like this "As you give so shall you receive".

As our awareness expands we are able to understand many of the principles of life and how to work in harmony with them to create whatever we chose in the external world.

As you know, we are all automatically evolving in this direction but there are many things we can do to accelerate our own evolutionary process.

If this concept is new to you, you can start by simply taking a few minutes each day to just relax. Become quite and still and just be in the silence. Another option is to spend some time in nature and pay attention to the natural beauty of the plants, the trees, the sky, the water, the birds and animals.

Do anything, even if just for a few minutes each day, that removes your attention from the concerns of your external world.

Meditation is a most profound way to connect more deeply with your inner world.

But, you can start by just by asking yourself some questions.

Chapter 4

QUESTIONING

"The important thing is not to stop questioning.
Curiosity has its own reason for existing"

Albert Einstein

S TOP – AND ASK YOURSELF SOME very important questions about your life and the world around you. You know the answers, but you have to stop all your external activity and take the time to listen carefully to your own internal wisdom.

We seldom ask ourselves these important questions. We are programmed to look outside ourselves for the answers we seek and accept other people's beliefs.

Taking time to stop and consider these questions and beliefs, for yourself, could make a huge difference in your life and the world around you.

You may want to start a journal for recording your answers to these important questions. It could be beneficial to stop after asking each question and write down what you think about the subject. Then to help you get more clarity, read your answer

Belief = your "stories"

again and ask yourself, whos answer is this? Is it what you really think deep inside yourself or is it something that you have learned from someone else and simply believe? Then, take one more look and ask yourself if it is true. Do you know for a fact that this is true? How did you form this belief? Did you hear this idea from your associates or the media? Did your source know for sure that it is true or is it just someone's opinion?

As we question ourselves we may learn a great deal about how we form our beliefs and realize that we have accepted things we have been told without questioning them.

You may want to think about how your beliefs come to be. When we stop to think about it, most of the time, our beliefs are formed from the information we have been exposed to --- there could be other information that contradicts this information that could be just as convincing, but we didn't hear that information. So, we form our opinions (beliefs) with the limited information that we happened to receive. On some level we know that we don't know the whole story but we are content to form an opinion as though we did. In fact, we don't know the whole story about anyone or anything other than our own personal story.

If we discover that we really don't know if our beliefs are true, it keeps us open to considering other possibilities. Otherwise our mind is closed, which doesn't leave any room for new discoveries.

Remember that your beliefs and attention are a creative force.

As you read this book it should become abundantly clear that what you think matters.

These first two questions are things to ponder as you read

through this book and arrive at your own conclusions about the following subjects that affect us all.

1. Why am I here?
2. How do my thoughts and beliefs affect my experiences and the world around me?

Note — I am not suggesting that I know the answers to these questions. I am just providing food for thought. The important thing is that we just ask the questions and consider possibilities.

Let's now look at our beliefs and accepted world beliefs about the following subjects. If we had all known that all of us are connected and a part of a larger body then we would have never experienced our first subject.

WAR

War is complex, in the past whenever we thought of war we probably believed that it was too complex for us to understand. Therefore, we thought someone more knowledgeable about politics and war probably knew why it was necessary. Since wars have been going on throughout history, we assumed that war was necessary, so we never challenged that belief, until recently.

Thousands of people are now asking why do we fight, why do we go to war? Has war ever brought about the desired results? Has anyone ever really won a war? Why do we stop fighting? What happens when we stop fighting?

Let's look at some possible conclusions people have arrived at after asking these questions. First, yes, war is too complex for us to understand. Furthermore there is no one smarter than us who understands wars. The human intellect is incapable of clearly understanding complex systems. It can follow a cause and effect relationship so far and then gets lost in the complexity. Therefore, if one continues on in the maze of complexity, guessing takes over.

The only way we can intellectually understand a complex system is to take the root of it and follow it back to its source. Let's try that with war. Let's move it from this huge complex thing, and bring it back to something smaller that we can more easily understand.

War is similar to a street fight, it just involves more people, who are better organized and have more artillery. Now let's bring it down to a personal level. Why do people fight? Fighting, disagreement, disharmony are all a result of a difference of opinion, or in other words, different beliefs.

The major belief that underlies most wars and fighting is the belief that supply, whether it is land, oil, money or support for our beliefs, is limited. It is the belief that someone else has something that we need or want, or that they are keeping us from fulfilling our needs and desires. Is this true? It certainly seems to be, but what if we knew that to be a totally false belief?

Does war ever bring about peace? Many people die and many more are injured and/or disabled for life. What could we possibly win that is worth that? Since death and destruction happen on both sides, how could we say anyone won?

We are told that we go to war only in self-defense. This indicates that fear is the basis of war. We build up arms to create fear

24

in others; we are attacked because others are afraid of us, while we say we are afraid of them. Sounds like a vicious cycle doesn't it?

Why do we stop fighting? Anyone stops fighting only when they are convinced that fighting **will not** accomplish their goals. Has anything changed? Probably not, both parties continue to have the same beliefs and the same needs, desires and fears.

What if we discovered that what President Roosevelt told us so many years ago was totally true? I am referring to the famous lines in his inaugural address, **"The only thing we have to fear is fear itself"?** Would there be any reason to go to war?

Chapter 5

IS FEAR IN CHARGE?

There's nothing I'm afraid of like scared people
Robert Frost

WHY IS IT THAT WE are taught when we are children that we should not fight? And, as adults, if we are caught fighting in public, we will most likely be arrested. "Thou shall not kill" is one of the Ten Commandments that most people respect as a rule for living. Killing another is considered murder, and an individual can be put to death or go the jail for life for killing someone. Anyone who engages in fighting at any level is considered a low class citizen or a criminal. We are taught that intelligent, civilized people find more appropriate ways of working out their differences. Yet all of this is seen from a totally different perspective when it is a country that has a problem with another country.

Then we are told it is our duty and the most honorable thing we can do is to fight for our country. Young men and women are asked to fight and kill other young men and women. It all seems a bit confusing, doesn't it?

In the Vietnam War many young men gave up their home and country to protest this illogical reasoning, or should I say, lack of reasoning? They refused to allow authority to force them to do things that they knew within their own hearts and minds were not in their best interest or the best interest of their country. They stood up to authority, and some of us remember hearing their chant, **"Hell no, we won't go".** Those who refused to go to war knew there would be consequences for making this choice, but they faced the consequences to help us all see how totally out of line this request was, and how society was trying to control their beliefs.

This led to a change in how the military operates. Shortly thereafter, the armed forces became all-volunteer. It became clear that young people would no longer blindly follow what they were told to do. They had begun to think for themselves.

Thousands of people protested the Iraq war, and for the first time in history, two 2008 US Presidential candidates announced in a debate that war was no longer acceptable.

When people stop to think and refuse to be controlled by fear, something wonderful happens. They discover new possibilities.

On a level that is not obvious for most people, a true awakening is taking place. People are taking responsibility for themselves, their thoughts, beliefs and actions, and are discovering a whole new way of viewing the world.

What do you think about war?

RELIGION

Many people today are even questioning religion, the one thing that many of us never dared to question.

Has religion also been controlling us through fear?

Are the religions of today serving our needs? Exactly what role does religion play in our lives?

In the past we thought of religion in much the same way as we thought about war. We thought it was too complex for us to understand and we believed that someone else understood these complexities and we were being guided by these people in the right direction for our greatest good.

What happened to the place we once thought that we could go to for comfort and inspiration? For years now priests around the world have been discovered molesting young children who trusted them and came to them for spiritual guidance. Numerous ministers around the country are getting caught doing all the things they preach against, like lying, cheating and extortion.

There have been popular books on the market in recent years about how the Catholic Church has hidden manuscripts that were contrary to their doctrine, and forbid their members to read any literature that expressed differing opinions.

Is what we have believed about religion in the past true?

On the New York Times best seller list we find books like *The God Delusion* by Richard Dawkins, professor of the Public Understanding of Science at Oxford University. And *God is not great: How Religion Poisons Everything* by Christopher Hitchens, who was hailed as "one of the most brilliant journalists of our time" by the London Observer. Both men are pointing out all of the horrific damage that has occurred in the name of religion, all the wars, the deaths and suffering.

Studies show that most people who are affiliated with an organized religion are simply following in the footsteps of their parents. Have you ever questioned the value of religion?

We have many good honest religious leaders with a strong belief in the value of religion, who are trying their best to revitalize it. Will it work?

These are just questions to consider.

What if we discovered that we live in a perfectly ordered universe where everything that exists has a purpose, and when that purpose has been fulfilled it is replaced by something of a higher order?

What do you think?

MORALS/ETHICS

Is religion responsible for moral or ethical behavior? That seems applicable only if one is still being controlled by fear. Many people today are discovering that moral or ethical behavior is the only behavior that works to bring about the desired results.

Almost every day in the news we see people who have chosen to act in unethical ways are now being caught and brought to justice for their choices.

What if we discovered that morals and ethics are not about right or wrong, good or bad, but about what works? What if we discovered that it is true that only moral and ethical behavior will bring about what we desire? What if we discovered that this behavior is the way to get results and that only moral and ethical people will be the leaders of tomorrow?

What do you think?

WEALTH/MONEY

What is wealth? Does just having a lot of money make one wealthy?

Money rules the world, right? But, do we really want to rule the world? When we think that we want to be wealthy, what does that mean, what do we really want? Money is something that we use to exchange for something else, so what do we want to exchange our money for? Many times we believe that money will bring us security or happiness. Is this true?

We may need money, but it is not the money itself, but what we plan to do with the money, that is valuable.

It is only a belief in lack that keeps us bound to thinking that making money is the most important thing that we can do in our lives. For most of us it may be a lack of clarity about what we really want.

What if we discovered that we have the innate ability to fulfill all of our needs and desires right within ourselves?

Maybe then money wouldn't be as valuable as we once thought it was. What do you think?

RELATIONSHIPS

Do we know what is best for all people in terms of intimate relationships? Are other kinds of relationships acceptable, other than the kind we have been programmed to believe fit all people? Could it be that individuals should be free to choose the kind of relationships that work for them?

Should all marriages last forever?

What is the purpose of marriage?

My experience with all the people I have worked with over the years is that the greatest desire people have is to be happy. When are you happiest?

What role do relationships play a in your happiness?

Maybe it is time to really get clear about what is important to you. It could be very valuable to take the time right now to prioritize your life in terms of what's important to you.

Actually, the most important relationship in your life is your relationship with yourself. Do you care for yourself? Do you get enough sleep, eat right, exercise and take responsibility for your own health? Do you take time for your own personal growth and development? You know that no one will or can do it for you. Your choice about this relationship will affect every other relationship in your life including your partner, family, work and ability to provide for yourself and others.

How do relationships come to be?

What if we discovered that all of our relationships are for our personal growth? And that we attract people into our lives for the growth and development of both parties. And those relationships begin when the relationship is appropriate for our growth, and ends when its purpose has been fulfilled.

Can we create peaceful, harmonious relationships with everyone in our lives?

SEX

What happened to, "sex is a bad thing", and one should not engage in it until after marriage? Of course, once the minister/priest/whomever said, "I now pronounce you husband and wife", it all of a sudden becomes a wonderful thing.

Old beliefs about sex, like everything else, have been challenged. The sexual revolution started openly in the 1960's. And we have been actively experimenting with sex ever since. Some people have learned a great deal while others have gotten caught up in other beliefs that were just as destructive and unrealistic as the old.

In chasing excitement and fulfillment, without any understanding about what sex actually is, people have discovered most often an emptiness and lack of fulfillment. It has also been used as a tool for getting something else such as love, money or other things. Does that work?

What if we discovered that sex is an exchange of energy, and that when we engage in sex we are merging our energies and taking on characteristics of our partner? What if it is like taking on characteristics of another person when a body part of another person has been transplanted in our body?

How does sex really work in our lives and what are the right choices for us to make about it? Does everyone get to choose for themselves? What do you think?

Chapter 6

WHO'S RESPONSIBLE?

ENTERTAINMENT

Responsibility is the thing people dread most of all,
Yet it is the one thing in the world that develops us,
Gives us manhood or womanhood fibre

Frank Crane

W HAT IS ENTERTAINMENT? IS WHAT we are seeing on TV and in the movies today what we really want to see? Why have TV and movies become obsessed with violence and death? Is our entertainment a reflection of collective consciousness?

It seems to me that actual up-lifting shows, that we once saw, have given way to shows of horrific violence.

How does the kind of entertainment we engage in affect our bodies and minds? When we watch a movie, TV show or the news, we are experiencing these events as though we were there and our bodies are responding to these experiences. When we watch these shows we are in a constant state of "flight or fight", as described in my e book, *Understanding Stress*. This stress

builds up in our nervous systems, causing us to feel edgy,
and irritable. It also makes us less capable and blocks our
to experience inner peace. It damages both the mind and body.

Go to my web site at <u>www.unlimittedfutures.org</u> to download a
copy of my stress e book and discover what the stress in your
life is doing to your mind, body and your experiences.

What if we refused to participate in entertainment like this that
is hazardous to our health?

What if we discovered that entertainment could be uplifting and
fun instead of frightening and overwhelming, and that we can
demand that it is?

MEDICAL/HEALTH CARE

Millions of people today are interested in alternative health
care. Are there better and more effective ways of caring for
our health than what we have known in the past?

Who is responsible for our health?

What can we do to improve our health?

What if we discovered that most illnesses can be prevented?

AGING

Is illness a natural outcome of aging? Could there be a way
whereby we could stay healthy and fully enjoy life for as long
as we are here?

What if we discover that we have been given incorrect information about how we age?

Dr. Deepak Chopra tells us that the human body is constantly replacing all of its cells, and that we have a totally new body every seven year. How can a body be aging when it is constantly renewing itself?

What if we discover that we simply get what we expect? What if we discover that our beliefs create our experiences? Those experiences in turn validate our beliefs and keep us expecting something that is not at all necessary with regards to aging?

What if we discover that there is an easier, more efficient, more effective and more enjoyable way to live our lives throughout our entire stay here on earth?

SUCCESS

What is success?

Does your bank account reflect your degree of success?

If you were totally successful what would your life look like?

What price have you paid for your success?

Has your "success" cost you your health or special relationships?

It seems to me that a good definition of success would be to accomplish your life goals. However, in order to do that we must first know what those goals are.

If your life could be just the way you would like it to be what would it look like? (This is a very important question to consider)

In light of your answer to the above question - are you successful?

Many people today are realizing that the way we have measured success in the past is totally unbalanced and unsustainable. It leaves us with a big gap between what we have thought of as success and the lives we actually want to live.

The following is a story from a colleague, Dr. Eric Kaplan, who wrote this story in his book *The 5 Minute Motivator*. I thought it was a brilliant example of the American way of looking at success.

One day an American investment banker was at the pier of a small coastal Mexican village when a small boat with just one fisherman docked one afternoon. Inside the small boat were several large yellow fin tuna. The American complimented the Mexican on the quality of his fish and asked how long it took to catch them.

The Mexican replied, "Only a little while."

The American then asked, "Why didn't you stay out longer and catch more fish?"

The Mexican said, "Why, with this I have more than enough to support my family's needs."

The American then asked, "But what do you do during a normal day?"

The Mexican fisherman said, "I sleep late till about 10, have a little coffee with my wife, play with my children, then I go fish a little. Then I come home, clean my fish, and take siesta with my wife, Maria. When I awake, we stroll into the village each evening where I sip wine and play guitar with my amigos. I have a full and busy life."

The American scoffed, "I'm a Yale MBA and I'm positive I could change your life. You should spend more time fishing and with the proceeds buy a bigger boat: With the proceeds from the bigger boat you could buy several boats. Eventually you would have a fleet of fishing boats. Instead of selling your catch to a middleman you would sell directly to the processor, eventually opening your own cannery. You would control the product, processing and distribution. You will eventually need to leave this small coastal fishing village and move to Mexico City, then Florida and eventually New York where you will run your ever-expanding enterprise."

The Mexican fisherman asked, "But how long will this all take?" To which the American replied, "15 to 20 years."

"But what then?" asked the Mexican?

The American smiled, laughed and said that's the best part. "When the time is right you would announce an IPO and sell your company stock to the public and become very rich, you would make millions."

"Millions?...Then what?"

The American said, "Then you would retire. Move to a small coastal fishing village where you would sleep late, fish a little, play with your kids, take siesta with your wife, stroll to the village in the evenings where you could sip wine and play your guitar with your amigos."

The Mexican just shook his head and walked away.

This story gives us a glimpse into how ridiculous and how programmed many people have become in defining success.

When I was in my 40's, my husband and I were vacationing at a lovely resort on one of the Caribbean Islands and noticed a very large yacht docked there. The couple who lived on the yacht was obviously retired and very wealthy. They were probably in their late 60's, but looked much older. We watched their life style which consisted of partying most of the night every night. They set up a huge bar on the top deck of the yacht and people came over every night to party with them. During the day they just laid in the sun waiting until the people came over in the evening. Their skin looked like leather. For the week we were there this was their daily life.

My husband and I agreed that if this is success and the pay-off of the great American dream we were very happy that we opted out.

We all need a certain amount of money to live comfortably, but how much money do you need? Research has found that after we have enough money to live comfortably, that more money doesn't contribute much to our enjoyment of life.

How much money is enough? The answer to that question varies tremendously among people. For some it is very little and for others no matter how much they have it will never be enough.

There, of course, are no correct or incorrect answers. This exercise is to help you get in touch with the thoughts and beliefs that are producing your external world of experiences.

Chapter 7

MORE AWAKENINGS

There is an inmost center in us all,
where truth abides in fullness.
Robert Browning, nineteenth century poet

W E ALL HAVE OPPORTUNITIES TO discover a better way of life, but if we let those opportunities pass by, Nature usually gives us a wake-up call. Sometimes we are so busy that we don't even notice the wake-up call, but Nature is persistent. We get another one and another one until it gets our attention.

In her book *"Thrive"* Arianna Huffington, Co-Founder, President and Editor in Chief of the Huffington Post Media Group, tells us about her own wake-up call. She found herself in a puddle of blood on the floor. She had collapsed at her desk from sheer exhaustion. This finally got her attention.

As a result of that wake-up call, Huffington has written an excellent book that can help us all see through the illusions about success. In "Thrive" she writes "Wherever we look around the world, we see smart leaders – in politics, in business, in media --- making terrible decisions. What they are lacking is not IQ, but wisdom."

Where do we find wisdom? Could it possibly be right within ourselves?

Huffington continues; "I believe the second decade of this new century is already very different. There are, of course, still millions of people who equate success with money and power --- who are determined to never get off that treadmill despite the cost in terms of their well-being, relationships, and happiness. There are still millions desperately looking for the next promotion, the next million-dollar payday that they believe will satisfy their longing to feel better about themselves, or silence their dissatisfaction. But in the West and in emerging economies, there are more people every day who recognize that these are all dead ends ---that they are chasing a broken dream".

Have you had your wake-up call yet?

Pay attention and your wake-up call may not be as drastic as Arianna's.

LEADERSHIP

When we look around and observe all the systems that are not working today, for instance, government, the legal system, education, big business, etc. The list could go on and on. As we observe what is happening in the world around us, it becomes clear that what we need are leaders who can see beyond the limits of the intellect.

Who will be the leaders of the future?

be the people who can multi-task? Do a dozen things
? People who get the least amount of sleep because
, are always working?

I don't think so. What if we discovered the leaders of the future will be people who have created optimal health for themselves. Optimal health, of course, brings one to the top of Maslow's hierarchy of growth, self-actualization.

As Maslow clearly describes, self-actualized people are highly intuitive. They can see the big picture and how all the parts are connected and fit together. He says they are highly creative and most are making a special contribution to the world around them. Self-actualized people will clearly see why the old paradigm no longer works and how to create altogether new systems for business, government and all kinds of organizations.

They are aware that they can create whatever they chose, and they chose to express their unlimited abilities for creating a much different and better world for all of humanity.

AWAKENINGS FOR CULTURAL CREATIVES

In 1997, sociologist Paul H. Ray, Ph.D. published an eight year study of the American culture. In it he states, "A major change has been growing in the American culture. It is a comprehensive shift in values, world views, and ways of life. It includes nearly a forth of American adults, or 44 million people."

Dr. Ray divided the American population into three groups of world views. He defined the first grouping as *Traditionalist*, people who are invested in non-change and a desire to move back into the past. That group included 56 million adults, or 29% of the population.

The second world view he defined as *Modernist,* which represents 47% or 88 million adults. He described these people as placing a high value on personal success, consumerism, materialism and technological rationality.

The third group he calls *Cultural Creatives.* This is a new emerging and rapidly growing culture, which in 1997 represented 24% of the American culture or 44 million adults. Cultural Creatives' interests focus around personal growth, including psychology, spirituality, self-expression, self-actualization, alternative health care and social concerns. Ray states that Cultural Creatives are affluent, well-educated and open-minded.

In 2005, Ray and psychologist Sherry Anderson updated the research. They found that in the 8 years between the research projects that the Cultural Creative group had grown from 44 million in 1997 to 50 million in 2005, and that they are growing at a rate of one percent a year. Ray and Anderson also observed that millions from the Modernist camp are now crossing over to this new world view. It appears the same changes are taking place in Western Europe.

Ray and Anderson predicted that the Cultural Creatives could be the dominant culture within five to ten years.

If we look at these groups of people we can clearly see where they are on Maslow's hierarchy of growth chart in terms of what needs they are focused on, or motivated by. The traditionalists are still focused on their need for belonging. The Modernists are focused on their need for respect and self-esteem and the Cultural Creatives are focused on autonomy. The Cultural Creatives have evolved to the need to take responsibility for themselves and the world they are creating. These people are awakening to the realization that our old beliefs and ways of functioning have not brought about what they really want in life. They are questioning old beliefs and are discovering greater and greater possibilities.

Chapter 8

JOINING THE REVOLUTION

There are two ways to be fooled. One is to believe what
Isn't true; the other is to refuse to believe what is true
Soren Kierkegaard (1813 – 1855), philosopher

SCIENTISTS AROUND THE WORLD ARE discovering a whole new science. They are discovering that the world simply doesn't work the way we believed it did.

Lynne McTaggart, an American investigative journalist, published her book *The Field* in Great Britain in 2001 and in the U.S. in 2002. McTaggart traveled around the globe meeting with physicists and other top frontier scientist in Russia, Germany, France, England, South America, Central America and the U.S., and corresponded with many other well-known highly credible scientists in other countries. She discovered a small but cohesive community of top-grade scientists with impressive credentials, all working on some small aspect of the same revolution. She reported on their work and found that their discoveries were incredible. What they were working on seemed to overthrow the current laws of biochemistry and physics. They were indeed discovering a new science, a new view of the world.

The prologue of her book is entitled "The Coming Revolution". In it she states "We are poised on the brink of a revolution – a revolution as daring and profound as Einstein's discovery of relativity. At the very frontier of science new ideas are emerging that challenge everything we believe about how our world works and how we define ourselves".

McTaggart continues; "Researchers discovered that the Zero Point Field contains the blueprint for our existence. Everything and everyone is connected with one another through this field in which all information from all time is said to be stored. Ultimately, everything from man to matter – can be traced back to a collection of electric charges that are continually in contact with this endless sea of energy. Our interaction with this field determines who we are, will become and have been. The field is the alpha and omega of our existence."

If you are interested in a full scientific understanding of what this book is all about I highly recommend that you read Lynne McTaggart's book, *The Field*.

In my own discovery or peak experience, I could see and understand the workings of what the scientist are calling "The Field". I could see that everything in the entire universe is connected. Separateness is only in form. The universe is one pulsing interactive energy field. I saw the source of creation as pure potential. We could call the source anything, like God or the Unified Field.

I do not use the word God, because people have too many beliefs about God, and my intent is to communicate, so I want to use words that do not have preprogrammed meaning in our minds. However, since we seem to have some programming about most words, I chose to call the source Love. Love has a much more expanded meaning in this context than what we usually think of as love, but love is the closest thing that we can experience to the source. This Love is a different kind of love. It is not emotional; it simply is everything in existence.

I could see that when the source moves or begins to express itself energy is created. This energy is directed and formed by intelligence, which is also an aspect of the source. Therefore, the first law of nature or principle of life that you need to understand is that **"Everything in existence is Love expressing intelligently through energy."**

We are energy and so is everything in existence. All energy is intelligent and indestructible. It is everywhere. It is moved and formed by intelligence. On the physical level we are energy and on the mental level we are intelligence. We create our own experiences with our thoughts and attention. Thought, beliefs and attention directs and forms energy.

I could clearly see that there are laws of nature of principles of life that are non-changing. They govern how we create our experiences, and how we collectively create world experiences.

One of these laws is the law of attraction and it is always working in our lives. This non-changing law determines what we experience. It attracts the energy to us to create whatever we believe in and are focusing our attention on. I usually call it the law of attraction and repulsion, because it also repels other energy. This is how we create our own experiences.

There are, of course, many laws of nature or principles of life that are helpful for us to know. We work with 7 of them in our courses. But you can see how the process works with just the understanding of these three.

1. Everything in existence is Love expressing intelligently through energy.
2. Thought (beliefs, attention and intention) directs and forms energy.
3. The law of attraction and repulsion. (We attract what we believe in and repel energy that doesn't fit our beliefs)

Another valuable principle to understand is that "Beliefs are simply information that we have accepted as truth". When we realize that it is our beliefs that create our experiences, most of us realize that we have been programmed to believe many things that must be changed in order for us to create the kind of life we want.

We can clearly see that what we believe determines our choices; our choices determine our actions, which ultimately determine our experiences. However, changing beliefs requires a major focus, and most often a strengthening of our nervous systems, which, of course, is also necessary to help us move beyond fear.

Fear is simply a belief in an undesirable outcome. As you can see, the two go together and both must be changed in order to be able to create a better life.

People everywhere are discovering some of these principles. For many years, we have been hearing the saying "What goes around comes around" or "What comes from you returns to you." What we are really referring to here is the principle of attraction. Many times the intellect is not capable of detecting how this works, because it works in a longer time frame than the intellect can follow.

Even the Golden Rule is a principle of life. We usually hear it as "Do unto others as you would have them do unto you". This sounds like the right and good thing to do. However, this is not the full understanding of it. The law actually goes like this "As you do unto others it shall be done unto you". It is the law of attraction in action. Again the time frame doesn't always allow the intellect to see it.

Another revelation I discovered was that time and space is for our convenience in experiencing the way we experience. Time and space do not exist in the field.

Many of these discoveries are now being discovered by people around the world. We are seeing evidence of some of the discoveries in movies, books and also on television talk shows.

For example, the film "What the Bleep," in which they tell the story of a person's life, and a number of highly respected scientists describe what is happening in scientific terms. Another example is the film "The Secret" which features the law of attraction. Both films are available on DVD, if you'd like to check them out.

Chapter 9

MOVING TO A NEW AGE – THE CONCEPTUAL AGE

Agricultural Age (farmers)
Industrial Age (factory workers)
Information Age (knowledge workers)
Conceptual Age (creators and empathizers)

I N 2005, DANIEL H. PINK wrote *A Whole New Mind: Moving from the Information Age to the Conceptual Age.* He starts the Introduction of his book with these words. "The last few decades have belonged to a certain kind of person with a certain kind of mind — computer programmers who could crank code, lawyers who could craft contracts, MBAs who could crunch numbers. But the keys to the kingdom are changing hands. The future belongs to a very different kind of person with a very different kind of mind."

He also states that his book describes a seismic, though undetected shift now under way in much of the developed world. He says, "We are moving from an economy and a society built on the logical, linear, computer-like capabilities of the Information Age to an economy and a society built on the

50

inventive, emphatic, big-picture capabilities of what's rising in its place, the Conceptual Age".

When I heard Daniel Pink being interviewed on CNN some time ago, I was delighted with his understanding of what is happening in the world. He explained it in terms of left brain and right brain functioning. I agreed that this is a perfect metaphor for describing where we find ourselves in the evolutionary process of our growth today.

We now know that consciousness is not just in the brain, it is everywhere, but this seems like a good metaphor for talking about the two aspects of ourselves. It is actually a way to talk about our inner and our outer worlds.

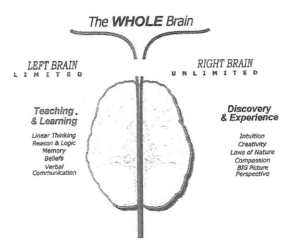

As illustrated above, the left brain is responsible for linear thinking, reason and logic, analysis, memory, beliefs and verbal communication. Our everyday functioning, for the most part, is a result of our reliance on left brain activity. Most of our educational system has been designed to develop these abilities, and most people have been _unaware_ of the fact that a more expanded awareness is possible.

We have been so busy living in our left brain world that few people dared to ask whether there wasn't something more. Abraham Maslow asked this all important question, and dared to pursue it. He found all of the right brain abilities described above clearly demonstrated in the self-actualized people that he studied.

Right brain capabilities include intuition, creativity, receptivity and inventiveness. Also included in right brain abilities is the ability to see the big picture and understand complex systems. It is being able to spontaneously experience an awareness of how parts of the whole fit together and affect each other.

Most of us have been aware that some people seemed to be more intuitive, but we as a society, have given very little credence to intuition. Since our left brain cannot grasp the concept, we have virtually ignored right brain abilities until recently. Now, however, people are searching for more fulfilling ways to live their lives and many have discovered that these abilities do indeed exist. These resources are within each of us and we can develop them.

Right brain abilities are developed in a totally different way than left brain abilities. The left brain can be taught. It responds and expands on the information that is delivered to it. The left brain, however, is **limited** to what it has been taught or experienced. The right brain, on the other hand is **unlimited.** Therefore, in order to reach optimal health and functioning we must develop our right brain abilities.

Developing our right brain makes a huge difference in how we see the world and function in it. In fact, right brain development opens up a whole new world for us, one we were not capable of even imagining in the past.

The right brain cannot be taught, it expands through personal discovery. Therefore, in order to discover our right brain abilities we must remove ourselves from experiences that keep the left brain in control.

The left brain is an outer functioning system designed for exploring and interacting in the outer material world. The right brain is an internal functioning system which allows us to be in touch with our deep inner resources. Our left brain defines us by the experiences in our lives. Our right brain knows that we are much more than what we experience.

Left brain activities allow us to do what we DO in the material world. Right brain activities give us access to the Source of creativity, the capabilities of genius and infinite possibilities.

If we do not develop our right brain functioning, we can get lost in the experience of living our lives. When we have not developed our right brain abilities we believe that life "just happens" and all we can do is react to external circumstances. Our left brain is too limited to understand how life works; consequently we simply buy into other peoples' beliefs.

Only intuitively can we see the big picture and how all the parts fit together. Only intuitively can we understand the laws of nature that govern all aspects of the material world. Only intuitively can we know how to work in harmony with these principles and create the lives we dream of living.

Bobbie Stevens, PhD

Since intuition is something that our "left brained" society is beginning to accept, we find people trying to teach intuition, which is impossible. There is no way that the **limited** left brain can fathom **unlimited** intuitive knowledge. We develop our right brain by removing ourselves from external functioning and focusing our attention within ourselves. We train the mind to become quiet and still and allow the space to receive intuitive understanding.

We need a well-developed left brain and right brain to be fully functioning people. We want to be whole brained. Verbal communication is the domain of the left brain. The mode of communication in the right brain is intuition. Intuition allows us to see and understand huge amounts of knowledge, but we are unable to communicate that knowledge until we have been able to make the connection between the left and right brain.

Remember I told you that after my peak experience I couldn't talk about it for years. It took that long to make the necessary connection between the left and right brain which makes it possible to put words to the experience. In our courses we help people develop their right brain abilities, which give them a huge advantage in functioning in all areas of life, including business. We work with a process for developing the right brain abilities and also making the right brain/left brain connections. Unlimited Futures' courses are experiential.

A few years ago, the President of a corporation who was contemplating sending his entire executive team through our Executive Development Program, asked us if he could send one of his executives to experience our personal growth course first. The individual experienced the course and came away with great results. She said it was the best experience of her life.

We scheduled a meeting with the President of the company and the executive shortly after she had finished the course. At this meeting he asked her to tell him about the course. She told him that it was the most valuable thing she had ever experienced. When he pressed for more information she said things like, "I see things that I never saw before, the colors are so much brighter, everything is lighter and there is order." Needless to say he was not impressed. We had scheduled the meeting too soon after her experience and she had not yet made the right brain/left brain connection. Therefore, she could not verbalize what she had discovered in a form that would be understandable to left brain analysis.

Deepak Chopra describes this growing into higher levels of consciousness this way; (my comments in brackets).

State of Contracted Awareness: (I believe this would be when one is functioning from the limits of the intellect, left brain, only) Imagine that you're walking in a dark room with only the small flame of a candle to light your way. You keep stumbling and bumping into furniture and other objects that you perceive as obstacles. You feel isolated and separated from the world around you. This is the state of contracted awareness.

State of Expanded Awareness: (This would be when we develop our unlimited right brain abilities) Now imagine that you're still in the same dark room but someone has given you a flashlight. With more illumination, you can move around freely without the fear of tripping or hurting yourself. You can also see that everything that seemed like an obstacle has a clear purpose. You can beam your light around and see that there is a couch you can stretch out on, a shelf filled with wonderful books, and a stereo for listening to music. What appeared to be threats or barriers are actually opportunities. You feel connected to the web of relationships that links everyone and everything. This is the state of expanded awareness.

State of Pure Awareness: (Full Enlightenment) Now once again imagine that you're in the same room but this time all of the walls, including the floor and ceiling, are made of transparent glass and the room is flooded with sunlight. When you look outside you see that the whole world is your playground. This is the state of pure awareness. There are no problems and therefore no need for solutions. You are the creative, evolutionary impulse of the universe. You feel the wholeness and oneness of life. You are in the flow and so you play.

Pure awareness is a long way away for most of us, but we certainly want to start moving in that direction.

To be fully mature or a fully functioning person we must develop both the left and right brain and be able to connect the two. Both are essential to create successful and fulfilling lives. Most of us have been developing the left brain throughout most of our lives. A highly educated, intellectually brilliant person has not necessarily developed his/her right brain.

The right brain gives one a much more comprehensive understanding of the big picture or how all the parts fit together and affect one another. It also is responsible for feelings like compassion and a much expanded awareness of joy, peace and wholeness. Artists of all kinds are usually trying to convey their right brain intuitive understandings. We see this in dance, art, music and, of course, writing. There are left brained procedures to follow, but really great art comes from a deeper level within the artist.

All new discoveries and inventions originate as an intuitive thought in the mind of someone. First the thought comes, and then it must be verified in the material world. This is what has happened in the minds of scientists and inventors around the world though out time.

Scientists were amazed to discover, in double blind studies, that the observer influences the observed or, in other words, the thoughts or beliefs of the researcher affect what he/she discovers. They found that objects big enough to be seen lacked form until they were observed. (Thought and attention directs and forms energy)

Scientists around the world are providing us with a truly new science. Yet, we still have a vast number of scientists who refuse to see the evidence. This is not just stubbornness; it is a reflection of where they are in the evolutionary growth process.

One of my students said to another student, "I know Bobbie wants us to become self-actualized, but I don't want to be self-actualized. I just want my life to be better." My first reply to this was another question, "How much better do you want your life to be?"

Yet I understood the dilemma. As we evolve through Maslow's hierarchy of growth, we are not able to see beyond where we are. We can look back and understand the different levels we have experienced, but we do not have anything that allows us to relate to experiences that we have not yet had.

Maslow's work has not been given the recognition that it deserves because there has not been enough people in our society who understood it, but that is now changing.

Chapter 10

WHY CHOOSE SELF-ACTUALIZATION

The goal of education...is ultimately the self-actualization of a person, the becoming fully human, the development of the fullest height that the human species can stand up to...

Abraham Maslow,
Twentieth century American psychologist

W E HAVE OBSERVED THAT THE self-actualized person has developed both left and right brain abilities. They have been willing to let go of the belief that left brain functioning (reason and logic) is our only way of accessing knowledge. They have learned to become quiet and still and tap into their intuition. Self-actualized people have greatly expanded their way of accessing knowledge. They are aware of the unlimited nature of this knowledge, and are able to live their lives on a whole new level of understanding and functioning. They are able to intuitively see the big picture. They can see how life works and understand the perfection, order and harmony of the universe.

The self-actualized person is no longer motivated by needs. They know how to fulfill all of their needs and desires right within themselves. They are clearly aware of the connection between all things and know how to move and direct energy to create whatever they want.

In psychology, we call this state of functioning self-actualization. If we were speaking from a spiritual perspective we would probably call it cosmic consciousness or enlightenment. It is a clear realization that we are not separate from anyone or anything else. We are at one with all, and that there is nothing outside of, or separate from us.

Growing in Self-Actualization

Self-actualization is just the next step in our growth process, and we grow in this awareness just as we grow in all of the other levels of growth that we experience.

Self-actualization starts from a deep desire to know our selves, to understand why we are here and how life works. If our desire is strong enough, we find the answers to these questions right within ourselves. We discover our ability to intuitively receive knowledge.

We become aware that we are not separate from anything, that everything in existence is connected and interacting. We begin to see that there are laws of nature or principles of life governing how we create our own lives and how we collectively are creating the world.

We have a completely different world view than what we had in the past. We know that life doesn't work the way we once thought it did. And what we have accomplished in our lives has been done the hard way, simply because we did not understand how life works.

We find ourselves literally living in two different worlds at the same time. We know that there is no separateness, but this is our challenge.

As we grow we are usually surrounded by people who do not know what we know, and our greatest desire is to share what we have discovered with them. Life is so much better, easier and more fun from here, but it is almost impossible to communicate what we have discovered. It is like going on vacation, seeing wonderful new sights and having great new experiences, and trying to share what you are experiencing with friends back home.

The self-actualized person still remembers all the programming (other people's beliefs). They know these beliefs are not true, and they must be very strong not to fall back into their old way of thinking. Their challenge is to integrate all of their new discoveries into their daily lives. Self-actualized people know that their beliefs create their experiences and living from a different understanding is a lifelong process.

Timing

What we are focusing most of our attention on determines where we are in our growth cycle. There are no distinct points of change from one level to the next; it is just a shift in interest and desire.

The speed in which we grow differs tremendously from one

person to another. It seems to me that stress plays a major role in how much energy we have and how fast we grow.

We grow as a society as well as individually within our society. The world is evolving at a much more rapid pace than it has in the past. We can see this in the number of discoveries and inventions that have taken place in the last 50 years. Studies show that we have seen more inventions and discoveries in the past 50 years than we had in the previous 100 years, and more in the past 100 years than in the 500 years before.

For the first time in history, larger numbers of people are experiencing self-actualization. Until recently, it was just a word that most of us did not understand or could not even stretch our imagination to believe was possible.

According to Paul H. Ray's cultural studies, approximately one third of our population is rapidly moving in this direction. We are clearly on the brink of a major paradigm shift and a giant leap in the consciousness of humanity.

HOW WE EVOLVE

Let's take a look now at how the evolutionary process works.

We are all growing, but we do not grow in a straight up direction. Our growth is more in a bell shape.

There are three forces influencing us at all times. We will call the first force Growth or the progressive force. That is the upward wave; we all have a need and desire to grow. The second force is one of Maintenance; there is also something within us that wants to maintain the status-quo. The third force we will call the Destructive force or wave. The old must go to make room for the new. Each of these forces plays a role in our growth. They are all influencing us at all times but one of them dominates our thinking at any given time.

When we are discontent with the present circumstances we want change, but we don't really want to change ourselves. We usually just want others to change. If others would change everything would be better. Is this true?

At some point we finally realize that for outside circumstances to change we have to change. Only at this point are we ready to fully embrace the progressive (growth) upward cycle.

When we are satisfied with the situation or our outer circumstances, the maintenance force takes over and it is very strong. We still feel the need to grow, but we really want to hold on to what we have. We are afraid of change. Giving up what we have or, are now experiencing, means venturing into the unknown. Fear takes over, and depending on the condition of our nervous systems, we are either capable or not of making that leap. This is true for all of us.

If the growth force is strong enough in us and we really want change we realize that in order for real change to take place we have to give up what we are experiencing now. Only when the present situation gets uncomfortable enough are we willing to let go of the old in order to make room for the new life or situation.

Letting go of the old is the next essential step before we can grow again. All three forces play a role in the growth process.

We observe the fear of change most clearly with addictions. We know we want to give up the addiction. We know why we should give it up but our nervous systems simply are not strong enough to make it happen. So we hold on to it as long as it is possible to tolerate. Only when it becomes unbearable are we willing to move to the next step of giving it up and starting a new growth cycle.

We display this reluctance to change when we stay in a job that is not fulfilling, for much longer than we know we should.

On a collective level we see it in terms of continuing to use systems and practices that are no longer effective. Many times it is easy to see that what worked well in the past is no longer working, but we hang on to the old until it becomes totally ineffective and we are forced to make changes.

I remember years ago I worked as a sales representative for a temporary employment agency. I called on companies to tell them how our services could benefit them. And I was amazed at the reason many of them gave for not trying it. Their explanation was, "We just have never done it that way". To them that was a perfectly good reason why they wouldn't try it.

We must discover what doesn't work before we are willing to let go of the old and try something new.

It is important that we understand that all three forces are, and must be, active at all times. This is simply how we evolve.

This evolutionary process is always playing out in our personal lives and it is also experienced in organizations, governments, nations and the world.

Let's now take a look at how this evolutionary process has played out on the world stage and where it could be leading.

PART TWO

MOVING TO THE
WORLD STAGE

Chapter 11

WHAT LIFE COULD LOOK LIKE AFTER THE TRANSFORMATION

*The new way of seeing things will involve
an imaginative leap that will astonish us.*
John S Bell (1928-1990) quantum physicist

WE KNOW THAT THE TWENTIETH century will always be remembered for the great advances made in technology. And I believe the twenty first century will always be remembered for the advancement in human consciousness.

Let's now take a look at what we might read in a history book about the twenty first century. Let's say we are reading this book at the beginning of the twenty second century. Let's see how things could have changed, and how it all unfolded.

At the beginning of the twenty first century people around the world were becoming restless. Those living in nations that had been governed by dictators for centuries refused to continue to follow. People were so determined to become free, they were willing to give up their lives for their freedom, and many did.

There were uprisings in countries around the world and a determination to overthrow dictatorial governments. There was much blood shed, but in the end, the dictators were thrown out and the people began learning how to govern themselves.

At the end of the twentieth century Bill Clinton was the President of the United States. During his 8 years as President, the country was at peace. He cut spending on defense and balanced the national budget, which had an all-time high deficit when he took office.

Al Gore was the Vice President in the Clinton administration, and ran for President at the end of Bill Clinton's term. However, George W. Bush ran against him and it was a very tight race. So tight that they didn't know for weeks who won the election. The Supreme Court of the United States finally decided that the presidency would go to George W. Bush.

Many people couldn't believe what had happened, but what they discovered later was that Al Gore had a very important job waiting for him. He was one of the few people who understood what was happening to the environment, knew that something must be done to restore the health of the planet, and that it would take everyone to do it.

He took on this job, and, for the first time in history, the entire world came together to cooperate in the accomplishment of their mutual goal of saving their planet. He began to rally people around the world to do their part in cleaning up the environment. This, of course, had far reaching consequences in so many areas of their lives. This project took many years and involved people around the world but in time it was accomplished, as more and more people become self-actualized.

The George W. Bush administration played its role in the evolution that was taking place. At the end of his presidential term they were in the middle of two wars, the surplus that was left in the federal budget had been depleted and the budget deficit became the largest in history. Wars were raging, the economy was in trouble and people were suffering.

This turn of events got people's attention. It was the country's wake-up call. Many people were questioning many old accepted beliefs.

In the next election held in 2008, the people wanted change and huge numbers of people turned out to participate in the election process. People who had never participated or paid much attention before became involved. These trying times caused people to question many things that they had not questioned before.

For the first time in the history of the nation, a woman, Hillary Clinton, and a black man, Barack Obama ran as major candidates for President of the United States. At this time, people realized that the world was changing very rapidly. Both blacks and women had been discriminated against throughout the nation's history and this caused people to ask another question. Why do we discriminate against people? It seems that as a nation they were starting to let go of the fear and small thinking that had created discrimination.

Barack Obama wrote books laying out his concerns about politics and all aspects of how the government was being run. He campaigned on "Change". Obama promised to change many of the ways government was operated. By this time, most people were aware the old systems weren't working anymore and they wanted someone in the presidency who understood that, and would be a catalyst for change. He attracted huge crowds at his rallies, and many people started to trust him and believe that he could and would make the changes necessary to move the country in a new direction.

He ran against Republican John McCain in the general election. Obama won the presidency, and he appealed to people around the world.

Each of these presidents played their role in the evolutionary process. The majority of the people voted for each of them, reflecting the collective consciousness of the people at that time.

Not only the United States, but the entire world was in the midst of the largest financial crisis since the Great Depression of 1929. Unemployment was running at the highest rates in many years, the stock market was crashing and financial markets had come to a halt. Huge numbers of homes were in foreclosure all around the country, and businesses of all kinds were going into bankruptcy. The picture for their future looked grimmer every day and the entire world was gripped in fear.

It was truly magical how worldwide fear turned into hope the day of Obama's inauguration. People could feel a change in the energy. This brought about a shift in the mind-sets of people around the world.

Everyone sensed that a new era had begun. It seemed that the United States and indeed the entire world was experiencing hope.

Yet underneath this forward, progressive movement during the

Obama administration in the United States, many people around the world were suffering and were falling deeper and deeper into fear. This showed up very clearly in the 2016 election when the world received another very loud wake-up call.

This got the attention of people around the world and more and more people began questioning, and came to the realization that if the change they were looking for ever came to be, it would be up to them to bring it about. More and more individuals begin to discover the power they had within themselves to make a difference in their own lives and the world around them.

More and more people realized that they had to take responsibility for themselves and people seemed to be ready to do that. They became more introspective and willing to look at themselves. They wanted to understand how this crisis came about and they knew they had to find a way to make the changes they wanted in their own lives. They knew something had to be done and it was up to each person to discover what to do and make their own individual contribution to creating a better world.

As a result of all the questioning some people begin to realize that much of what they believed in the past simply was not true. Many people begin to think that there had to be a better way and started searching for a deeper understanding of life. More people started experimenting with yoga and meditation, and started having experiences that they had never had before. Some became highly intuitive and word got out that intuition is real, and that it was a human potential that could be developed.

Books and articles were written about right brain abilities. For years people had been talking about the fact that people used only a small portion of their potential, but around this time more people were becoming aware of the fact that there was enormous potential lying dormant within everyone. In the past they had mostly been aware of intellectual functioning, (reason, logic, analysis, etc.) Their educational system developed these intellectual (left brain) abilities. People discovered that educating the right brain was not a teaching/learning process as with the left brain. It was an inner process of discovery.

Those who pursued right brain development discovered a whole new world. They discovered abilities they never had before. Not only did they become highly creative and receive knowledge intuitively, but found they were able to clearly see the big picture, understand complex systems and see how all the parts fit together. They could see and understand things that had completely eluded them before.

They begin to see and understand the laws of nature that govern how each person creates his or her own experiences and how they collectively create world experiences. They became aware that it was their beliefs that create their experiences and that their beliefs were not necessarily true. In fact they became aware that beliefs are only information that have been accepted as true, and that they can be changed, thereby changing external experiences.

These people became aware that they lived in a perfectly ordered universe and they could see how it works. They knew that in the past they had been going in the wrong direction in seeking answers to their questions. They found that love, joy, happiness and all the things they had been seeking were right within themselves. They became aware of their true identities and knew themselves to be an expression of the source of all of creation. They awakened to the realization that they were not separate entities, but that everyone and everything were expressions of Love, Intelligence and Energy. They realized that what they had always been seeking was to know themselves.

It became clear to these people that every aspect of life is governed by laws of nature or principles of life. And when these laws or principles are understood and one works in harmony with them they could create the kind of lives they wanted for themselves. It was also obvious that right brain development was essential for their future success. People begin to realize that when their thoughts and actions were not in harmony with nature, they simply created consequences that did not provide the desired result. They just provided opportunities for growth. They had not been able to see this using their left brains, because the cause and effect did not play out in a time frame that the left brain was capable of following.

These people began to understand that they lived in a perfectly ordered universe and all they had to do was to be receptive to the knowledge of the laws of nature and function in harmony with them to create whatever they choose. However, until they were able to live in harmony with the laws of nature, life was just a learning process.

As more and more people grew into self-actualization, all aspects of their lives changed. First there were only a few people who had discovered how to develop their right brain abilities and move into self-actualization. They clearly tried to help others, but all they could do was to show people the way. They learned that everyone must go through their own discovery process in order to move into a more advanced way of functioning.

Over the decades as more and more people became self-actualized, it changed every aspect of how they lived their lives.

Due to this evolution in human consciousness the entire world was changed.

Chapter 12

HOW RELEGION WAS AFFECTED

*Truth is not introduced into the individual from
without, but within him all the time.*
                                    -Soren Kierkeguard,
                            nineteenth century Danish philosopher

H ERE IS HOW RELIGION CHANGED. Around the turn of the century
they noticed that fewer and fewer people were attending
churches or any place of worship. Many religions were having
internal problems, so they believed that once they cleared up
these problems that people would return to church.

Around that time, many books were being published challenging
religious beliefs and there was a big controversy going on in
the schools about what children should be taught. The question
was; how to reconcile their belief in God with what the scientific
community has discovered?

They had evolved through many myths about God, and had long
since let go of the belief that God was a man with a long white
beard sitting up in the sky somewhere, blessing some people
and punishing others. They also let go of beliefs that the devil

was a man with a long tail and a pitch fork, but it wasn't until people discovered how to develop their right brain abilities did they understand that they were not separate from God. In this process people discovered God within themselves. They became aware that religions were about beliefs and they were no longer interested in other people's beliefs, they wanted to have their own experiences. As people became more aware of their own spiritual essence, they became content with their own spiritual awareness or state of Being. At this point religion gave way to spirituality.

People discovered the part of themselves that connected them with the knowledge of the spiritual aspect of humanity. As more people moved into self-actualization or enlightenment they become aware that God is all there is. They knew God as Love, Intelligence and Energy, the source of all of creation. They were also able to see that all of creation is governed by non-changing laws of nature or principles of life.

Scientists around the world were making new discoveries and for the first time in history the objective world and the subjective world came together.

What they discovered is that there have been enlightened people on earth, who knew this, throughout recorded history. These people tried to share their knowledge and understanding with others, but most people were not capable of understanding it.

They realized that all sacred writings had been an attempt to help people move toward enlightenment. Most people in the past were simply not capable of understanding the message that the enlightened ones were trying to bring to them. This lack of understanding accounted for the many different religions around the world; they were just people's interpretation of what they thought they were being told.

Most of the Ministers, Priest, Rabbis, etc, had their own awakenings and moved into more advanced states of consciousness. They discovered their purpose and many of them helped others to make their own discoveries.

They no longer had a conflict with the scientific community since everyone was discovering the same things. They just came to it from different directions.

Therefore, religion as it was in the past no longer exists. There are still a few churches, mosques, synagogues, etc, in some parts of the world. But there are other places where people gather to discuss spiritual meaning which has replaced most religious establishments.

"Many things brought the down fall of religions. At the beginning of the century many religious leaders were found guilty of doing the very things they were preaching against. Without going into all the scandals that happened in different religions let's just say that people lost faith in the religious leaders. In addition to that many scrolls that had been buried for centuries were discovered. These scrolls proved that present day records were incomplete, and clearly pointed to certain people and groups who had used the scriptures to control the masses for their own purposes.

They discovered scriptures that had been used for centuries, had been misinterpreted in their many translations. People could only interpret them from their own level of understanding, and often did not understand the people of the time when they were written, therefore causing many inaccurate interpretations.

All these things helped people to start looking within themselves rather than trusting religious leaders. Therefore religion played its part in the evolution of consciousness.

"Religions had traditionally focused on preparing for a better life after death, and for the most part, people did not realize that sacred writings were trying to show them a better way of living their lives in the present time. What sacred writings brought, was a code of ethics or guidance for living, which people professed to live by. However, many believed that these ethics were just for those who wanted to be a good person or wanted a better life after death. What they came to understand was that the scriptures were trying to tell them about the laws of nature that govern everything.

For example, the Golden Rule, "Do unto others as you would have them do unto you". They discovered that this is more than just a kind thing to do, but that it is a law of nature that goes like this, "As you do unto others it shall be done unto you".

This is just one of the fundamental laws that they misunderstood. Society had to experience what does not work before they were willing to give up their old beliefs and start opening their thought to a higher level of understanding.

What they discovered is that they lived in an orderly universe that is governed through unchanging laws or principles. Every choice they made had an absolute consequence that they could not see using the left brain. They had to grow by experiencing the consequences of the choices they made that deviated from the principles of nature.

They had always had free choice, but could not always see what the consequences of their choices would bring. What they now know is that whatever happens is always governed by universal intelligence and is always for their growth.

People are still curious about what happens after death. It is almost universally accepted that life is eternal. Scientists have a theory which they call the string theory. In more common terms, it means there are different dimensions of life. No one knows how many, but they now understand that they are spiritual beings having a human experience. When that experience is finished and the spirit releases the body they realized that it simply moves ones consciousness into a different dimension of life. They began to understand that it is something like taking a nap, and when they awaken they realize that they did not die, they are just having a different experience.

They discovered that heaven and hell are just states of mind that everyone creates for themselves while living on earth.

Chapter 13

THE CHANGES IN BUSINESS AND THE ECONOMY

To believe your own thought, to believe that what is true for you in your private heart is true for all men.
-Ralph Waldo Emerson

L ET'S NOW TAKE A LOOK at what happened in business and the economy as a result of this shift in consciousness.

As people became more enlightened and could see and understand the laws of nature that governs everything they realized that ethics are not just principles they needed to adhere to if they wanted to be a good person.

They witnessed what happened to those who did not act ethically and tried to increase their personal gain by lying, cheating and stealing. As a result people begin to see that there are non-changing principles that govern everything and there is no possible way to change those laws or get around them.

Since their left brains were limited, these wrong doers couldn't see the results of their choices. To the left brain it appeared that these schemes would work, and they did seem to work for a time, but inevitably in time the consequence of their choices showed up.

As a result of this growth process, people became aware of the fact that it was their thoughts and beliefs that create booms and busts – prosperity and recession or depression. They observed that when the economy was at its peak, many people were making lots of money, and then someone begins to think "This is too good to be true. It can't last." In many cases these pundits were financial advisors. They started sharing their beliefs through their newsletters and soon the media picked up on this belief and spread it even further.

Fear then took over. Since beliefs guide actions, some people stop spending, others become afraid and decide to get as much as possible for themselves before the opportunities went away. These actions delivered exactly what was expected, a recession. Then, at some point someone believed that they could get out of this recession and experience prosperity again. This belief is shared with the public and the start of a new era of prosperity begins. They discovered that what happens with the economy is a direct reflection of collective consciousness.

When they were limited to left brain abilities only, they believed that individuals were separate and things just happened. They were unaware of the role people pay in creating whatever they experience, in business, on a personal level and a global level.

Once people faced the fact that they had problems in government and business, they knew there had always been a few people who were capable of creating something new, a better way to do things. Now they needed more of those people than ever before. It was time to finally take notice of what had been growing in their society for years — a group of people who had discovered how to develop right brain abilities.

Early in the twenty first century, some of these people showed up, creating a new kind of business. John Mackey, co- founder and co-CEO of Whole Foods Market and Raj Sisodia wrote a book entitled Conscious Capitalism explaining how to run a conscious business. In it they explained how some people understood, and began to practice a new way to run a business.

As other businesses observed how more enlightened CEOs, described in the book, were running conscious businesses they begin to realize that the old ways of running a business simply didn't work anymore and knew they had to make some changes.

They finally realized they all needed to develop their right brain abilities. Most people knew intuition existed, but few understood the power of it or realized that it could be developed.

Organizations desperate for knowledge on how to change their way of operating, started sending their employees to courses that developed their right brain abilities, (intuition, creativity and innovation).

As more and more people developed their right brain abilities and became self-actualized they saw the world from a totally different perspective and everything changed. The way they ran their businesses changed, and the way they interacted with others changed.

As people became aware of the power and abilities they had within themselves, and how everything is connected, they realized that their past view of the world was very limited. They had a whole new world of understanding to work with and create from.

It became clear that bigger is not better, and many large businesses broke up into smaller companies. In order to provide the best quality, people needed to relate to their work. Work needed to be meaningful for them and something they took pride in doing.

People were no longer willing to work just to make money after they discovered their inner ability to create. People became aware that everyone has a purpose. They asked to know their purpose, and discovered the work they were meant to do. They worked to express themselves and make a contribution to the lives of others.

Money no longer rules the world as it had in the past. As more and more people became self-actualized, they realize that money is just a means of exchange, and that everything that they needed or wanted is made of energy, as is money. They realized that there are laws of nature governing how everyone can create whatever they choose in their lives. People became aware that much of what they wanted to experience in their lives was not material --- it was energy --- and self-actualized people knew how to work with energy to create whatever they wanted.

As they continued to evolve people became aware that "supply" is not limited. They discovered that they have the ability to create whatever they want; therefore it is not necessary to hoard large amounts of money. They simply create the amount of money they need for whatever they want to do with their lives. This, of course, varied a great deal depending on what one choose to do, but there was no longer the striving for money that existed in the twentieth century.

They observed that self-actualized people are not motivated by money. They are motivated by the opportunity to express their talents and abilities and make a contribution.

They discovered that it was their beliefs and focus that moved and formd energy into whatever they choose. They also discovered that money doesn't buy many of the things that they found important in their lives. Therefore, people's life styles changed tremendously. People began to live much more balanced lives than they had in the past. They lived happy, fulfilling lives, which included work.

There were no longer very wealthy or very poor people. Most people learned how to create what they wanted, and most lived very comfortable lives. Everyone worked and greatly enjoyed using their talents and abilities to provide goods and services for others. People work because they enjoy working, not because they have to work.

As people became more enlightened they became aware of the perfection of everything. They discovered someone wants to do every job that needs to be done. It is just a matter of connecting the right person with the right job.

Chapter 14

HOW RELATIONSHIPS CHANGED

*The region of truth is not to be investigated as a
thing external to us....It is within us....
Consciousness, therefore, is the sole basis of creativity*
Plotonius, third century Greek philosopher

LET'S LOOK AT HOW RELATIONSHIPS between people including gender relations changed.

In the twentieth century, there were major concerns with discrimination and they overcame that.

They discovered that discrimination was a result of fear. People were afraid of anyone who was different from them either in appearance or behavior. As people evolved their nervous systems became stronger, their minds became clearer and they simply out grew that kind of fear. In the past people were unable to see the perfection or order in which life unfolds`.

When people believed they were separate from the rest of the world and had to protect themselves from each other and outside forces, fear reigned supreme. As people evolved, they could see that we are all a part of one perfect universe, and that every person has a reason and a purpose for being. At this point they started to appreciate the differences in people, and were clearly aware that these differences were essential for the good of everyone.

They began to understand why these differences are important, and how they complement each other. Once they started developing their right brain abilities and were able to see the big picture or the perfection of the wholeness, in which everyone is a part, they began to understand the value each person brought to the whole.

It became clear that they needed people with different perspectives, which they found in different races, nationalities and gender. It became obvious that they needed to capitalize on these differences by becoming aware of what those differences were, then put the person most qualified for a particular job in that position. This was easy once they had moved beyond fear.

"When we looked at what was happening at the beginning of the century, we were still totally unaware of the real differences between men and women, their inter-dependence, and what they each brought to the table.

In 2008, Dee Dee Myers, the former White House Press Secretary in the Bill Clinton Administration, wrote a book entitled *Why Women Should Rule the World*. In it Myers clearly described the differences between men and women in their perspectives and interest. She also discusses experiences in the work place, and the continuing discrimination against women. She quoted Dr. Luann Brizendine's research which proved that gender begins in the brain.

In her book *The Female Brain,* Dr. LuAnn Brizendine explained that male and female brains are indistinguishable in the weeks following conception. Then, at about eight weeks, the male baby gets a dose of testosterone, which literally begins killing off cells in the communication, observation, and emotion processing centers of the brain – and growing cells in the sex and aggression centers.

She says that the male brain is about 9% larger than the female brain, but both brains have the same amount of neurons. They are just packed in a smaller space in the female brain. In the areas of the brain that control language and hearing, for example, women have on average 11% more neurons than men. In addition, the connection between the right and left halves of women's brains is larger, and each of the hemispheres less specialized.

Scientists believe that this more connected; more integrated female brain allows women to process information from a number of sources simultaneously. This also increases the female's ability to receive information intuitively.

According to Brizendine, women have "outstanding verbal agility, the ability to connect deeply in friendship, a nearly psychic capacity to read faces and tone of voice for emotions and states of mind, and the ability to defuse conflict. All of this is hardwired into the brains of women".

Another study showed that the areas of men's brains that control action and aggression are predictably larger.

"For most of the twentieth century women were kept out of the legal profession because men thought they were too kind, too gentle to be good lawyers, that to be a lawyer you had to be tough-minded and rough-hewn" said Sandra Day O'Connor, the first woman to serve as a justice on the Supreme Court of the United States.

They now know that men and women are of equal value, but each bring different talents, abilities and perspectives. They now understand that every human being on earth has a purpose that only that individual can fulfill. Once they were able to see the perfection of Nature's creation on earth, and know their own wholeness, were they able to accept that we are all different and indispensable. And that everyone is here to help and serve each other. They now clearly understand that by being in touch with their purpose and cooperating with others, they all can fulfill their dreams and desires.

Chapter 15

LIFE STYLE CHANGES

I see my life as an unfolding set of opportunities to awaken.

Ram Dass, philosopher

WITH THIS WHOLE NEW PERSPECTIVE on life, people's life styles changed greatly. Let's look at some of these changes. The large cities of the twentieth century are gone. They now live much more peaceful and balanced lives. Most people live in smaller villages, and have many more small businesses. As explained earlier they discovered that bigger is not better. As more people developed their creative abilities, they wanted to express themselves in their own way. Many started their own businesses and family businesses became the norm rather than the exception.

Once people discovered that they had the ability within to create the life they wanted for themselves, they begin to leave big cities and move into the countryside, where they formed villages and some smaller cities. They connect with people around the world electronically, so they felt it was no longer necessary or desirable to live in big cities.

Men and women found that when each is capable of expressing their own talents and interests they could create very profitable enterprises. Many people work from their homes; in fact, most small businesses are home businesses.

They created life styles that support optimal health and fulfillment. A typical day would start with the entire family getting up after eight hours of sleep, going outside to get some fresh air, then returning to do an exercise routine for releasing stress and keeping the mind/body energy sufficiently refined to allow them to function in harmony with natural law. After their exercise program they all meditate.

The average work day is between four and six hours. They discovered that when the mind is strong and clear, it is not necessary to spend as much time at work. They now accomplish just as much in four to six hours of work as the people of the twentieth century accomplished in eight to twelve hours. They find great satisfaction in their work, and they also have time to engage in many activities that they enjoy. They also understand the importance of taking care of themselves and living a balanced life style. They take full responsibility for their health.

They now understand that the planet is a living system and understand that they are cells in the body of the universe. The universe and our bodies operate in a similar way, each having systems that allow them to function perfectly. Once they became aware of the perfection of natural order they were able to start functioning in harmony with it.

Their food supply greatly improved since family farms came back into vogue. Sometimes several families work together on a farm, and there are also some village farms. Most of their food is raised locally, using practices that were once called organic farming. They do not use pesticides or chemical fertilizers that damage the soil and the water. All farms adhere to organic practices so now they just call it farming. There are usually enough farms in the area to provide food for surrounding villages.

They understand that everyone has a purpose in life. They simply go within, ask to know their purpose, and listen for intuitive guidance. They understand how their desires lead them to fulfill their purpose and make their contribution to the world. They now know that one job or line of work is not any more important that another. There is someone who enjoys doing every job or task that needs to be done and every job is important in some way in helping people. There are no longer repetitive or mindless jobs. They have robots to take care of such tasks. People work in professions they enjoy.

Since they realized that they were not separate from each other and that they were each a part of the greater whole, it changed everything. When people were caught up in their egos (believed that they were separate from the rest of the world), they felt they had to prove themselves, and be better than others, smarter, richer, etc. They now know that they are each unique. They know that by developing their abilities they can make their contribution for the greater good of all. They realize that others have talents and abilities that they do not have. They provide products and services that make their lives better and everyone contributes to the good of all. One job is not better than the other, just different.

People still get paid in relationship to their ability to do their

91

Bobbie Stevens, PhD

job. There is still a difference in how people get paid, the fewer people who can fulfill a need, the more others are willing to pay for their services. However, money is usually not the motivating force that leads one to their profession or career. Most people are simply doing what they love to do.

Relationships have changed tremendously since discovering that each one has the innate ability to create whatever they chose. They get to work at what they want to do and so does everyone else. Cooperation and mutual respect has replaced competition. Men and women cooperate with each other to accomplish something more than either could have accomplished alone. Businesses cooperate with one another to provide something more than they could have provided separately.

With this understanding, everyone is happy to let any person who wants to work at a particular job do it. They know that if someone else does a job they are interested in doing, they will find something more fitting for their abilities that is equally fulfilling for them.

Their games are also different from the games of the past. They no longer play games that produce winners and losers. Their games are played just for the fun of playing. They are always trying to play to the best of their ability, but not to beat someone else, but to improve their own performance.

It is also really fun to take a look at their entertainment. The shows have meaning and are uplifting. Their news includes all kind of good news about the progress people are making and opportunities for people to come together to support projects of interest.

Chapter 16

CHANGES IN THE MEDICAL COMMUNITY

Every human being is the author or his own health or disease.

Buddha (c. 563 B.C.E. –c, 483 B.C.E.)

N OW LET'S SEE WHAT HAS happened in the medical community over the twenty first century. Since people are living such healthy life styles, what is there left for the medical profession to do?

In the twentieth century most of the education doctors received was about disease and malfunctions of the body/mind. They called this profession a health care system, but it really didn't have much to do with health. It was mostly about what to do when physical systems break down or are attacked.

Much of the education now is about health – how to create and maintain optimal physical, mental, emotional and spiritual health. Most people take responsibility for their own health. Much of what doctors do now is just work with people to help them understand how the body/mind systems function.

In the later part of the last century and the early part of this century people were already questioning the validity of traditional medicine. Dr Deepak Chopra, who was a medical doctor originally from India, played a major role in moving the world into a different mindset concerning medicine. He realized that medical science in the Western world didn't understand the mind/body/spirit connection. He knew there had to be a better way. Dr. Chopra left the medical field and devoted his life to informing the world about the mind/body/spirit connection. He helped them understand that they were all spiritual beings having a human experience, and that it all works quite differently from what they had believed in the past.

Doctors also begin to understand there was a huge gap in their previous understanding of health and the mind/body/spirit connection. More books began to be published on the subject. As they more clearly understood this connection the medical profession changed completely.

People began to realize that they had to take responsibility for their own health and began to have a clearer understanding of health and how it relates to all aspects of life.

There are still people who make bad choices relating to their health, but very few.

They seldom use drugs and surgery as they did in the twentieth century. They now know that the bodily systems are electromagnetic energy systems, and we simply need to keep the energy flowing freely. Much of the healing work is now done with energy regulation and light and sound therapies.

Chapter 17

CHANGES IN EDUCATION

I have never let my schooling interfere with my education

Mark Twain

N OW LET'S TAKE A LOOK at education.

After struggling through the first decade of the twenty first century it became clear that the educational systems were totally outdated and ineffective for educating twenty first century students. They had to completely restructure the system. Much of what students were learning was useless and what they really needed to learn was missing.

There were groups of people in the past that saw this and offered a more balanced view of education. Maharishi Mahesh Yogi brought Transcendental Meditation to the United States in the mid twentieth century, and it blossomed into a worldwide movement. Millions of people discovered the benefits of meditation. The TM movement also brought us an International University which was the first to provide whole brain development.

In the past only left brain education was provided in the schools. That was before people evolved to understand that the right brain or the spiritual essence of who we are, gives access to a whole new world of understanding and functioning.

The present educational systems provides for both left and right brain development which are developed in totally different ways. The left brain is taught and learns information about all aspects of life in order to implement the vision people have for their lives. The right brain connects people with the spiritual essence of who they are and allows them to see all possibilities. The right brain also connects people with their purpose in life and allows them to see the big picture or wholeness intuitively.

They discovered that only through the development of the right brain abilities were they able to know who they are and perceive the wholeness of life.

Once enough people were capable of whole brain functioning, they created a whole new educational system.

Chapter 18

SUMMARY OF THE CHANGES

All change is not growth; all movement is not forward
Ellen Glasgow

L ET'S NOW TAKE A LOOK at what has happened around the world
as events unfolded in an orderly way over the entire century.
Here is a summary of some of the changes that took place.

In the United States there were huge disagreements in congress
between the two political parties and it became increasingly
obvious that the two party system was no longer working. When
this system was created, it worked perfectly. Each party would
present opposing views. They would consider both points of view,
compromise and come up with solutions.

However, the beginning of the end of this system started
when competition became so fierce that the attitude became
"whatever you are for, I am against, regardless of what it is."
They had lost touch with any desire to create solutions for the
good of all. Egos, a belief of separateness, had blinded them to
what was supposed to be their purpose for being there.

Agreement on almost anything seemed to be impossible. Two strong opposing forces were at work, the desire to maintain the status que and the desire to grow. One group was desperately trying to preserve the old way of doing things while the other was determined to move forward.

Over time the progressive group won the day and, in time, brought them into a whole new world view or perception.

CORRUPTION

At the beginning of the century corruption was rampant all over the world including in the United States. It was in government, the legal system and in all areas of life including businesses of all kinds, financial institutions and medical organizations.

Then in the second decade of the century cameras popped up everywhere, and made it increasingly difficult to keep secrets. Government and business' electronic files got hacked and what was once secret was no longer secret. People complained about losing their privacy, but technology had taken over and people now had the ability to uncover corruption of all kinds.

Corruption, in many well-established organizations was exposed and many of those organizations went by the wayside. Gradually technology actually wiped out secrecy, and since corruption cannot exist without secrecy corruption also disappeared. It became clear the practices of the past would not work in the future.

In addition, more and more people were becoming aware of their connection with each other and with the wholeness of life.

At that point they began to wonder why they were keeping secrets from themselves.

Self-actualized people realized that all corruption came about due to the incorrect belief that we are separate from each other and the world around us. It was this one incorrect belief that was the basis of all corruption. Once they clearly understood, the new scientific findings that we are all connected and that what affects any of us affects all of us, everything changed.

It was clear to see that the old systems and ways of doing things were not working, nor would they ever work because they were based on an incorrect concept. They realized that it was time to take a good look at all aspects of their lives.

They reevaluated the reason and purpose of government. As they evolved they needed a new kind of government for a different kind of people.

A new species of people were evolving and they were able to create new forms and systems that suited their new world.

There was a worldwide awakening and people around the world begin questioning the status quo, and were no longer willing to simply go along with past beliefs and practices. They discovered that there was more to life than what they had understood in the past. People were searching for the deeper meaning of life.

Many self-help books and programs were created to help satisfy this desire. Some of them were helpful and some were not, but people were determined to discover the deeper meaning of life and understand what it is all about and how it all fit together.

Scientist around the world explored new concepts and theories. They even built the world's most expensive and complex experimental facility, to that date, to explore the Higgs theory. It was called the Cern Particle Physics Lab located in Switzerland.

Peter Higgs came up with a theory in 1964, seeking a way to discover the origin of creation or the God particle as it was called. The Higgs Boson Theory was proven in the Cern lab in 2012. Yet, there were still many unanswered questions and a desire to personally experience life on a different level than they had in the past.

People realized that there were some people throughout history who had perceived a deeper meaning to life and had lived their lives from a totally different level than what they had been experiencing.

Science flourished and they discovered things that completely reversed previous concepts of the world and how it works.

Once enough people clearly understood the wholeness of life and realized that everything in existence is connected, attitudes changed about almost everything. They understood that Nature was clearly in charge.

They also knew that the laws and principles that govern everything were absolute and non-changing. No matter how they tried to hang on to the belief of individual separateness, and accomplish things their own way, they saw that all their efforts just taught them that their concept was incorrect and ineffective.

As more and more people became aware of their

interconnectedness their vast legal systems began to diminish. As people became healthier their minds became clearer and they made better choices. Even people who didn't yet understand this, realized that every choice has a consequence and that consequence is the fulfillment of a law of nature. You could not get around it or change it. They realized that there are absolute laws of nature and they work the same every time.

Technology continued to expand and the creativity that came into the field was amazing. It changed the way they communicated and almost everything they had known in the past.

Early in the century a well-known talk show host, Oprah Winfrey, bought her own TV network and aired a show on Sundays called Super Soul Sunday. On this show she interviewed people who had experienced their own awakenings. Most of them were rich and famous people who discovered that the money and fame didn't bring them the kind of lives they wanted. And they discovered that there was much more to life than what they had known in the past. Oprah's guest had awakened to a much more rewarding and fulfilling life. These interviews were revealing and inspiring and as more people watched the show, the audience grew so that millions around the world became aware of greater possibilities, and wanted to experience those possibilities for themselves. She also teamed up with Deepak Chopra to help people learn to meditate.

Chapter 19

EQUAL VALUE BUT UNIQUELY DIFFERENT

The world will be saved by the Western woman.
Dalia Lama

AS PEOPLE REALIZED THAT THEY lived in a perfectly ordered universe, governed by laws of nature, they begin investigating their own nature. They came to understand the differences in the nature of men and women. They discovered that not only are they physically different but their entire way of thinking and functioning is vastly different.

This brought about a greater understanding between men and women. Once they realized that nature is in charge and that everything is in perfect order, they begin to understand that not only does each have a purpose in life, but each one is perfectly designed to fulfill their individual purpose. Each has talents, abilities and interests in fulfilling that purpose.

They also learned how to take a complex situation and follow it back to its origin to discover its true nature and purpose. They discovered that the female and the male brains function differently. The male brain is more left brain dominate and the female brain is more right brain dominate. The female also has a greater capacity for connecting the right and left hemispheres of the brain.

As they better understood the differences between the male and the female it became clear that each has different abilities and that they complement each other and both are necessary for the ideal functioning of most endeavors.

They also discovered that they had been entirely wrong in terms of which gender is the most qualified for what job.

The female nature is predominately nurturing, while the male nature is predominately aggressive and action oriented.

In examining interpersonal relationships they found that starting with the first relationship everyone experiences, the relationship between people in a family, gave them a much better understanding of what happens as that relationship expands to include more and more people.

The mother (female) according to her nature cares for, and directs the functioning of the family. The father (male) according to his nature aggressively protects and supports the family.

As they carried that relationship out into the world they could see that their approach in the past had been placing males and females in roles that their natures least prepared them for.

They finally came to realize that Love is more powerful than fear.

Fear had ruled the world in all of recorded history, but now they could see there is a better way. It became clear that all relationships work better when they are nurturing relationships where all people work together for the greatest good of all.

As they realized that they were not separate entities but that they were all connected and that they were only interacting within themselves, competition gave way to cooperation.

Women were recognized for their true value and took their place in higher offices in both industry and government around the world. They found that the most successful organizations had a female CEO (chief executive officer) and a male COO (chief operating officer). The CEO (female) who was most capable of seeing the big picture and how all the parts fit together, created the course the company would follow and the COO (male) implemented the plan. Working together with the realization that one was not more important than the other, companies became very successful. It was simply a matter of understanding the true nature and abilities of each gender.

Most of the Presidents have been females. Most world leaders today are females also, and countries' relationships with one another are totally different from what they were in the twentieth century. They now have what they usually refer to as the family of nations, in which their greatest interest is in supporting each other.

The world is at peace and prosperity reigns supreme.

Near the beginning of the century many people began having amazing awakenings. Some had near death experiences, where they died and crossed over to a different reality. These experiences validated the scientific concept that life is a series of cycles. All of existence originates form the Unified Field which is a field of pure potential. That potential manifests itself into the life we experience and then cycles back to the un-manifested field of potential.

Life span is much longer now than it was in the twentieth century. People in the twentieth century usually died serving in a war, from a crime, a disease, a physical malfunction or an accident. Now there are no wars, very little crime and most diseases have been wiped out. And because people are healthy their thinking is clearer, and they make fewer mistakes causing far fewer accidents.

Since they now understand that life is eternal, they know that when the body dies we simply return to the un-manifested (from our perspective) realm of life, carrying with us our memories and level of understanding as we continue to evolve.

PART THREE

WHERE WE ARE TODAY

Chapter 20

HOW WE GOT HERE

"It has become appallingly obvious that our technology has exceeded our humanity"

Albert Einstein

L ET'S LOOK AT HOW WE have grown farther and farther away from our true nature.

As you remember, we live in two different worlds – we have both an inner world and an outer world.

The outer material world has been accelerating and has now speeded up beyond our ability to cope. This is why we are seeing the huge jump in the evolution of human consciousness in this twenty first century.

As the world speeded up we begin to see changes coming about faster and faster. Technology brought on a whole new way of life and it kept changing. People found it very difficult to keep up with all the changes. The pressure to keep up became more and more demanding and people started spending more and more time in the outer world just trying to stay abreast of all the changes.

The demands of life in the outer world became overwhelming and people spent less and less time in their inner world.

The human nervous system is our means of transportation between our inner and outer worlds. It is also the communication system between the mind and body. As we tried harder and harder to keep up, our nervous systems were over stressed and damaged. This resulted in the nervous system becoming less and less capable of functioning properly. Our attention span began to decrease and in time it seemed like everyone had ADD (attention deficit disorder).

We became less capable of listening – we became less caring -- we went into a survival mode and forget that there is anything other than the outer world.

Our health suffered. Our relationships suffered. Yet, it seemed impossible to disconnect from the outer world. As people became more overwhelmed with the stress, and became less capable of even knowing their goals, much less attaining them, they began to feel powerless. People tried to relieve this feeling with excessive drinking, drugs, excessive eating, etc.

These things just accelerated the downward spiral. And the human nervous system, like external systems, can only handle so much stress until something has to give. This explosion showed up in obesity, addictions, self-destruction and violence.

Many people got caught up in the outer world and lost their connection to the depth of their own inner world where all the power lies. The outer world doesn't have creative power. It is just a reflection of what is happening in the inner world. If what's going on inside us is only exhaustion and confusion then that is what shows up in the external world.

Therefore, as people begin to lose their connection with their inner power their thoughts became very negative which reflected in the outer world.

There were groups of people who were predominately focused on each of the forces in the evolutionary process. One group was strong enough to make a different choice and stay focused on growth. Another group of people tried with all their might to maintain the status que, while another group got caught up in the destruction force.

This group felt totally hopeless. They were caught up in the external world and believed everything in their life had failed them and they were determined to destroy it all.

You have heard the phrase "He has lost his mind". That is exactly what happens when one becomes disconnected from their inner world. Mind is in the inner world and if we are unable to connect with it, we lose our ability to understand or function in the outer world, both physical and mental health spiral downward.

These evolutionary forces are balanced and work perfectly in healthy people, but when the nervous system is so damaged that one becomes disconnected from their inner world they can get caught up in the destructive force and are unable to see any possibilities for a future.

Chapter 21

A DIFFERENT CHOICE

No barriers, masses of matter however enormous,
Can withstand the powers of the mind —the
Remotest corners yield to them —all things
succumb; the very Heaven itself is laid open.
Marcus Munilius, Roman author, c. 40 B.C.

THERE WAS A GROUP OF people, and I was one of them, who decided to get off the merry-go-round. We did all the things we were told to do to create a life of success, happiness and fulfillment. Then at some point we found that even though we did what we were supposed to do, the fulfillment wasn't there. Instead most of us realized that something was missing. So we started questioning.

What went wrong? What was missing? Why didn't doing what we were told to do produce the promised results? What is life really all about? Could this be all there is? There must be a better way. Why do I have this empty feeling? What do I need to do?

At this point we became seekers. Here, my late husband, Dr.

Dean Portinga would give us this Bible quote "Seek and you shall find".

In our search, we begin going within. We begin asking ourselves these questions because we had already learned that the advice we had received from external sources had not worked.

As we learned to go within ourselves, we discovered our connection to the source of life. Here we found Love, joy, peace and power, all the things we were seeking. We realized that we had previously been looking in the wrong direction for the things that were most important to us.

This accounts for the many different self-help books, courses, etc that we see today. What, those of us, who have discovered a whole new way of life, want most is to share what we have discovered with others. We know it is possible for all of us to create better lives for ourselves and what affects any of us affects all of us, and together we can create a much different world.

What we are going through now is what my late husband, Dr. Dean Portinga, would call chemicalization. Through his many years of counseling and research he discovered the process that happens to individuals, organizations and countries when going through a major growth process.

The term came from observing what happens when you mix two opposing chemicals together. They immediately fight each other, a huge commotion takes place, sometimes even an explosion, but once everything settles down you have created something of a higher order.

He says chemicalization occurs when a person or group of people are no longer willing to maintain the status que and make a commitment to create something better.

Dean was almost 90 years old when he passed away January 1, 2016. He devoted his life to research and exploration. His curiosity kept him investigating everything from business to theology to science, psychology and personal growth. He was the director a research foundation for many years, doing research in the physical sciences, life sciences and the relationship between science and religion. He earned doctorates in both theology and psychology and was given honorary doctorates in divinity and education.

Dean wrote a paper on chemicalization that has helped numerous people understand the process. He explains why it is a good thing and why it is inevitable if we want to move forward. If you would like a copy of his chemicalization paper just go to his web site at www.spiritual-insights.net to download your free copy.

(foot note – I have been told that the word chemicalization originated with the founders of Unity which makes sense since he worked with them years before I met him)

Here is how Dr. Deepak Chopra describes what is happening in his book *Power Freedom and Grace*.

"In the broader sense of self, a critical mass of people in societies, communities, and institutions also determines the attitude of the larger bodies. When a culture has constricted identity, its emphasis is predominately on profit-making, ruthless competition, economic imperialism, extreme nationalism, military conflict, violence, and fear."

"If the critical mass of people were to express their expanded selves, not only would they spontaneously fulfill their personal desires, they would change the very way culture articulates itself. In such a transformed culture the emphasis would be on service rather than on greed, cooperation instead of competition, open hearts instead of open markets. Cultural hallmarks would be nonviolent conflict resolution, compassion, humility, peace, and social and economic justice."

How can we expand our awareness and express our expanded selves? I am suggesting that we can start by considering that our past world belief was incorrect. The belief that we are separate entities totally separate from each other and nature laid the foundation for the beliefs we have about all aspects of our lives.

Now that we know that everyone and everything in the universe is connected maybe it is time to change our entire world view. We can start by simply asking ourselves questions and know that we know the answers, now that we know we are connected with universal intelligence (all knowledge).

Here is what happened for me when I started questioning. As I mentioned before I had an awakening or what Maslow calls a peak experience. It was as though I was waking up from a dream even though I was wide awake. I woke up to a whole new world. I could see that Love is all there is - there is nothing in existence except Love. I could clearly see that everything in existence is Love expressing intelligently through energy. I could see that everything in existence is this oneness, and that -- I was at one with this wholeness. I knew there is nothing separate from it and I am a part of it as is everyone and everything else.

I felt totally at peace, whole, complete and perfect. For the first time in my life I knew that I was not a separate entity, but at one with everyone and everything in the universe. It was a wonderful new world where I understood how life and universe works. I realized that I had been freed from what is sometimes called the human condition.

Before, I was subjected to fear, doubt and all kinds of world beliefs, now I could see that practically everything I believed in the past was simply not true. Before I had no awareness of why things happened as they did or why we all struggled to understand life, but never succeeded. I had awakened to a wonderful new world. I knew my life would never be the same again and I was ecstatically happy.

I was in love, not the kind of being in love that we usually think about when we meet that one special person. But that is the closest I can come to describing what I felt. I then knew myself as love. I was in love with life and the wonderful realization that I was at one with this wholeness.

I could see that there are laws of nature or principles of life that govern how we create our own experiences and they just work the way they work, but if we understand them and live in harmony with them we can create whatever we chose.

Before this experience, I had no awareness of my role in creating my experiences or fulfilling my destiny. Things just seemed to happen that seemed beyond my control.

I could see that with the understanding of these principles, also came the ability to move and form energy into whatever I desired.

I, of course, began experimenting with this new understanding and started creating things just to see if I clearly understood how it worked. I could see that there was a creation process for creating anything, so I worked with this process to create a new business for myself, a townhouse, new furniture including a grand piano, a new car and another townhouse for rental income.

Next, I decided I wanted someone to share my life with. I was single at the time and lived alone. I worked with the seven step creative process and my understanding of the principles that govern how we create, and attracted into my life my perfect partner. We were happily married for over 37 years and had a wonderful life together.

If you would like to hear an interview that I did for Learning Strategies on the seven steps in the creative process just go to their web site at www.LearningStrategies.com/bobbie and download it for free.

I remembered my purpose here was to understand how the creative process works and share it with others. I had been very successful in creating what I wanted in my life, but in order to share this with others, I needed to know how this happened for me, what brought about this awakening, and how I could help other people have their own awakenings.

It took several years, but I finally understood what had happened. I then created Unlimited Futures to help others experience their own awakenings and discover the amazing potential we all have deep within ourselves.

I had moved into a totally new way of functioning, more advanced than I had ever dreamed possible. I realized a totally natural way of life, it is our natural state of being, yet few people ever experience it.

The reason few experience this level of functioning is because we have been programmed to believe the answers to all our questions must come to us from others. We keep focusing our attention on sources outside ourselves for the answers to our questions. When we are living in what is called the human condition we are totally unaware that the answers to all of our questions can be found right within ourselves.

I discovered a whole new life by simply starting to ask questions and believe that somewhere deep within myself I knew the answers. This same thing is also possible for you.

For many years I didn't know anyone else who had experienced anything like what had happened for me, but now I know there are many other people who have also had amazing awakenings. The experience seems to be somewhat different for each of us or, at least, we describe it differently, but the one thing that everyone seems to agree on is that it is the most real, natural thing they have ever experienced and it, of course, changes one's life forever.

We simply awaken to the realization of who we are. It is who we all are. We are all Love expressing intelligently through energy.

Each of us has a purpose for being here just like every cell in our bodies has a purpose. And when all the cells in our body fulfill their purposes it creates a fully functioning healthy body.

We know that all of the cells of our body work in harmony with each other when they are healthy and when one part of the body has a problem the other parts of the body come to their aid. This is clearly described in my book on stress. (you can get it free on our web site www.unlimitedfutures.org)

Our bodies are simply a replica of the larger body that we are all a part of.

Since everything in the universe is connected or a part of this larger body all of nature would support each of us in fulfilling our desires. Right?

When we have an intention to move our hand, it simply moves. It doesn't say "I don't know if that would be in my best interest", as would occur if it believed it was separate. Every cell in our bodies has their own intelligence and if it is healthy it knows its purpose and works in harmony with the other cells to simply respond to the guidance we give it through our intentions.

The universe works the same as our physical bodies when we live in harmony with nature (the universe) all of nature moves to manifest our intentions.

Universal intelligence speaks to us through our desires. This is how we know our purpose. We just have to go within ourselves to begin to understand the language of the universe and know our purpose for being here. And also know how to work in harmony with all the other parts of the universe to fulfill our purpose.

It has been my experience that is how it works. It doesn't work that way just for me but it works that way for others who also started asking questions and were lead to their own awakenings.

Chapter 22

PRINCIPALS THAT GOVERN HOW WE CREATE OUR EXPERIENCES

Consciousness is a source of self-cognition
Quite apart from and independent of reason,
Through his reason man observes himself, but only
through consciousness does he know himself.

--Leo Tolstoy

THERE ARE MANY PRINCIPLES THAT govern how it works. We work with seven of those principles in our courses but I think you can get a good understanding of how it works by just looking at three of these principles.

1. Everything in existence is Love expressing intelligently through energy
2. Thought, beliefs, feelings and attention move and form energy
3. The law of attraction and repulsion.

First we need to understand what scientists have recently discovered, which is what we have been talking about throughout this book. That is that everything in existence is connected. Once we understand this we know that we, everyone and everything else are a part of this universal wholeness.

We need to understand that everything on the physical level of existence is energy. Einstein proved this for us many years ago. And we need to understand that all energy is intelligent. And that everything in existence is energy in different forms.

Principal number two tells us how we move and form energy into our own experiences. The intelligent energy of the universe responds to our thoughts which include our beliefs and feelings. This forms the energy, and our attention moves the energy into these forms.

Actually principal number three explains the process that takes place. This principal is just like gravity, it is always attracting to us the energy necessary to fulfill our beliefs and where we are focusing our attention. It also repeals any energy that doesn't fit our beliefs. Therefore, we create whatever we believe and focus our attention on.

The principles just work the way they work so we can create wonderful thing or very unpleasant things.

Here I want to make clear that we do not create everything we experience. We do create most of our own experiences, but we do have experiences that the universe creates for us for our growth. In fact, everything we experience is for our growth. All of our experiences are leading us to deeper levels of understanding.

I couldn't leave you without exploring the choices we each have for making our contribution to collective consciousness which creates the external world we see around us.

The thoughts, feelings, beliefs, attention and intentions of every person on earth makes up collective consciousness which has created the world we live in today. Each and every person on earth has some degree of influence in collective consciousness.

So, what can you do to make a difference in creating our future world? How can you support the evolutionary process that is taking place in the world today? We each influence collective consciousness, so our thoughts, beliefs, attention and intentions will have an impact on creating the world of the future.

Since we are all connected and what affect any of affects all of us, we can make our contribution by simply creating wonderful, fulfilling lives for ourselves.

Chapter 23

WHAT WILL YOU DO?

*All religions, arts and science are branches of
the same tree. All these aspirations are directed
toward ennobling man's life, uplifting it from the
sphere of mere physical existence, leading the
individual toward freedom.*

--Albert Einstein

REALIZE THAT I AM asking you to challenge everything you have
learned in the past – to begin to ask questions and see if you
can discover the new life that is possible for you and all of us -
that is our Call to Action.

I am not asking you to just take my word for it. You can discover
these things right within yourself and this call to action is
asking you to begin that process for yourself as well as for the
betterment of all of us.

Now that you know that we have all been living our lives from
an incorrect belief, are you ready to challenge your beliefs? Are
you ready to discover and fulfill your purpose and be a part of
ushering in this new world?

Are you ready to discover the power you have within yourself to create the life you want for yourself regardless of what is going on in the external world around you?

By being all we can be, we can make a huge contribution to the creation of a much better world than what we are witnessing today.

If you are ready to explore your options and discover new possibilities we are here to help you.

You can find us at www.unlimitedfutures.org

Are you ready to experience the evolutionary process that is moving those of us who want to make a difference into a more advanced level of understanding and functioning?

All we need to do is fulfill our purpose here and when it is complete we get to go back home, see our loved ones that have gone earlier, and hang out in bliss again.

But for now we have work to do. Are you with me? Will you answer this call to action?

Einstein said, "The world is a dangerous place, not because of those who do evil, but because of those who look on and do nothing."

I am not asking you to march in the streets. What I am asking you to do is much less dangerous, much easier, more enjoyable and far more effective.

What I am asking you to do is to simply take 15 to 20 minutes each day to sit in silence. Find a place where you will not be disturbed and simply ask questions of your own inner wisdom. Then listen. You will receive intuitive guidance and it will change your life. And together we will change world experiences.

Will you make the 15 minute pledge right now?

I hope you have enjoyed reading this book and it has provided hope and food for thought. Please share it with all of your friends and associates. The more people who start asking questions and realize how powerful all of our thoughts are, the faster we all evolve and create a better world for all of us.

If you are still interested in investigating the scientific proof of these things, all the new science is amazing. You can find some of it in the suggested reading list. And, of course, you can Google it.

I offer this knowledge with the deepest gratitude for receiving it myself and the great privilege of sharing it with you.

SUGGESTED READING

Unlimited Futures: How to Understand the Life You Have and Create the Life You Want
Bobbie Stevens, Ph.D.

Spontaneous Healing of Beliefs
Gregg Braden

You Are the Placebo
Dr. Joe Dispenza

Power, Freedom and Grace
Dr. Deepak Chopra

The Spontaneous Fulfillment of Desire
Dr. Deepak Chopra

The Field
Lynne McTaggart

A New Earth
Eckhart Tolle

The Devine Matrix
Gregg Braden

Thrive
Arianna Huffington

The Universe Has Your Back
Gabrielle Bernstein

Happy for No Reason
Marci Shimoff

Conscious Capitalism
John Mackey and Raj Sisodia

A Whole New Mind
David Pink

Why Women Should Rule the World
Dee Dee Myers

The Female Brain
Dr. LuAnn Brizendine

Quantum Shift in the Global Brain
Ervin Laszlo

The Biology of Belief
Bruce H. Lipton, Ph.D.

You Are the Universe
Deepak Chopra, M.D. and Menas Kafatos, Ph.D.

The Leap: The Psychology of Spiritual Awakening
Steve Taylor

SCIENTIFIC REPORT

"Scientific Studies Report" provided by Ilke Angela MARECHAL
AnimaViva multilingue S.L.U.
Andorra

1) <u>Michael Talbot</u> *Mysticism and the New Physics*
Here spirituality, religion and science give rise to fundamental questions. Among other non-fiction books are *Beyond The Quantum,* and *The Holographic Universe.*

2) Great <u>Popularization</u> of Quantum physics has been achieved by both, scientists and scientific journalists: <u>Fritjof Capra, Ken Wilbers, John Gribbin, Paul Davies</u>, after some of the founding fathers of Quantum Physics had started to produce more simplified explanations of the deep underlying principles, their meaning and our understanding (Erwin Schrödinger, Albert Einstein, and more).

3) <u>Alain Aspect</u>, French physicist. In the early 1980s, ... he performed the elusive "Bell test experiments" which showed that Albert Einstein, Boris Podolsky and Nathan Rosen's (EPR) reduction ad absurdum of quantum mechanics, implied 'ghostly action at a distance'. This 'costly action' did in fact appear to be realized when two particles were separated by an arbitrarily

large distance (see EPR paradox). A correlation between their wave functions remained, as they were once part of the same wave-function that was not disturbed before one of the child particles was measured (Wikipedia).

Applied to cosmology we can say: in the original BIB BANG everything was in a single point. No matter how far our universe will expand from there: <u>Once in touch, forever in touch</u>, distances don't matter.

So, Einstein-Podolski-Rosen wanted to show that Quantum Physics (also called Quantum Mechanics) was absurd, and later John Bell theoretically went deeper in this matter, - but finally the <u>"Alain Aspect Experiments" proved practically the "unseparable oneness" of all matter.</u>

4) <u>Carl Friedrich von Weizäcker</u>, german physicist and philosopher, benjamin in the group of the founding fathers, came up (1975) in his equational work, with the concept of <u>Consciousness</u>, in a sort of downward causation, where in Aristotle's theory of the <u>four causes</u> (material, efficient, formal, and final) the 4th cause, the final cause or purpose, telos, is the most basic one.

Some titles of von Weizsäcker's tremendous work speak for themselves: L'Unity of Nature, L'unity of Physics.

5) Both, Poets and Writers, were always attracted by the New Ideas of a Unified Universe: among them poet Edgar Allan Poe (Eureka), Friedrich Dürenmatt (play writer), Edwin A. Abbott (Flatland), a beautiful fiction.

INDEX

A

abilities 14, 42, 51, 52, 53, 54, 55, 58, 71, 72, 73, 76, 81, 82, 84, 86, 88, 89, 91, 92, 96, 102, 103, 104

action oriented 103

actions 12, 27, 48, 73, 81

addictions 1, 63, 110

aging 35, 36

answers 6, 8, 12, 15, 21, 23, 39, 59, 72, 115, 118

Attention 5, 6, 14, 18, 20, 22, 40, 41, 47, 48, 54, 57, 60, 69, 71, 110, 118, 120, 121, 122

attention span 110

autonomy 14, 15, 16, 44

awakening 11, 13, 27, 44, 99, 115, 117, 128

awareness 5, 13, 14, 18, 19, 52, 55, 56, 59, 76, 115, 116

awareness and knowledge 13

B

balanced lives 84, 89

Being 2, 6, 8, 9, 15, 28, 29, 41, 49, 51, 52, 69, 75, 76, 77, 86, 88, 93, 97, 116, 118, 119, 124

Beliefs 6, 12, 15, 17, 18, 19, 21, 22, 23, 24, 25, 27, 32, 36, 39, 44, 46, 47, 48, 51, 53, 57, 60, 69, 72, 75, 76, 78, 81, 84, 99, 115, 116, 120, 121, 122, 123, 127

believe xvi, 2, 3, 5, 12, 14, 15, 17, 18, 22, 30, 31, 41, 45, 46, 47, 48, 53, 55, 61, 67, 68, 70, 80, 87, 118, 121

be receptive 73

a better way of life 40

131

K

Knowledge xiii, 4, 11, 13, 50, 54, 58, 59, 72, 73, 76, 82, 115, 125
knowledge and power 11

L

the law of attraction 47, 48, 49, 120
the law of giving and receiving 19
laws of nature or principles of life 9, 47, 59, 73, 76, 116
Leaders 29, 30, 40, 41, 42, 77, 78, 104
Leadership 41
the leaders of the future 41, 42
left-brain education 96
life x, xv, xvi, 2, 4, 5, 6, 7, 8, 9, 15, 16, 19, 21, 24, 26, 31, 35, 36, 37, 38, 39, 40, 42, 44, 47, 48, 49, 53, 54, 56, 57, 58, 59, 60, 62, 67, 71, 73, 76, 78, 79, 84, 85, 89, 90, 91, 93, 94, 96, 98, 99, 100, 101, 102, 105, 109, 110, 111, 112, 113, 114, 116, 117, 118, 123, 124, 127

lifestyles x
limited 22, 24, 52, 53, 54, 80, 81, 83
limits of the intellect 41, 55
linear thinking 51
listening 55, 110
love xi, 7, 32, 47, 48, 72, 73, 76, 92, 103, 113, 115, 116, 118, 120
Love expressing intelligently through energy 47, 48, 115, 118, 120

M

maintenance 62
a major paradigm shift 16, 61
make a big difference 3
male and female brains 87
marriage 31, 32
material world 18, 53, 57, 109
Medical Community 93
Meditation 7, 20, 71, 95
the mind and consciousness 9
mind/body/spirit connection 94
Modernist 43
money 6, 7, 24, 30, 31, 32, 39, 41, 81, 83, 84, 92, 101
moral or ethical behavior 29

CPSIA information can be obtained
at www.ICGtesting.com
Printed in the USA
BVOW06s1840240717
490140BV00009B/250/P

9 781504 382205